# THE SECRET ROADMAP FOR WORLD-CLASS CUTMEN AND CUTWOMEN

START YOUR CAREER IN MIXED MARTIAL ARTS, BOXING, AND MUAY THAI

ADRIAN ROSENBUSCH

*Foreword by*
ART DAVIE

Copyright © 2020 by Adrian Rosenbusch

All rights reserved. No part of this document may be reproduced or transmitted in any form or by any means, electronic, mechanical, photocopying, recording, or otherwise, without prior written permission of Adrian Rosenbusch except for the use of brief quotations in a book review.

Disclaimer: The information presented in this course and handout is not meant to be "medical advice." Adrian Rosenbusch, Fight Business Academy and its instructors, family members, and independent contractors are not medical professionals and make no claims as such. It is your sole responsibility to do your own research and follow all applicable laws in your jurisdiction. Adrian Rosenbusch, Fight Business Academy and its instructors, family members, and independent contractors accept no liability for the use/misuse of this information.

By buying or reading this book, you express your understanding and agreement with the following information:

The author, copyright owner, and publisher of this guidebook and its accompanying links, have used their best efforts in preparing this book. The author, copyright owner, and publisher don't represent or warrant the accuracy, applicability, or completeness of the contents this book, and they note that the information contained in this book is strictly for educational purposes. Therefore, if you wish to apply the ideas contained in this book, you are taking full responsibility for your actions.

For your specific circumstances, you should seek the advice of competent legal professionals.

The author, copyright owner, and publisher do not warrant the performance effectiveness or applicability of any sites listed or linked in this book. This book is not a substitute for legal advice, financial advice or medical advice. We do not represent or guarantee anyone will achieve the same results from using the formula outlined in this book. Each individual success depends on the individual's background, dedication, motivation, and interpersonal skills. The author, copyright holder, and members of Fight Business Academy, their families, and independent contractors do not guarantee any specific outcome.

www.fightbusinessacademy.com

ISBN: 978-1-7347868-1-1

*This book is dedicated to:*

*My lovely wife, Danyette who turns all my work up a million notches and is always in my corner;*
*My awesome little hippie kiddo, Ali, who is basically a Tim Burton character come to life;*
*My Dad who always kept my scientific mind sharp;*
*My Mom who is my #1 fan, my editor since I could type, and World's Best Mom/Grandma;*
*My supportive sister and brother-in-law who drove me to the airport for every one of my international gigs;*
*My friend Scott Bolan whose guidance has been amazing;*
*My friend Renzo Asparria of Hard Knocks Muay Thai for giving me a place to grow into the Cutman I am today;*
*My dear friend Swayze Valentine, the first Cutwoman in UFC history, and all-around impressive human being;*
*Every fight promotion and fighter I've ever worked with*

*This book is also dedicated to the memory of:*

*My niece Brianna Rosenbusch*
*and*
*Lauren Gaffney, daughter of Wendy Young*

*"Our time with you was too short. However short it was, it is still the most precious gift you could have ever given us. You will never be forgotten. We will honor your memory and share the love you shared with us. You were always loved and always will be."*

*- Adrian Rosenbusch*

# FOREWORD

When I was a boy, the *Boy Scout Handbook* was the official handbook for scouting. It was a descendant of Baden-Powell's original handbook, *Scouting for Boys*. That was, and still is, the key textbook providing information about camping, signs and signaling, scouting games and more. It contains everything a young person needs to learn to become a "well-developed, well-informed scout."

My good friend, Adrian Rosenbusch, has written the definitive book about becoming a Cutman/Cutwoman: The Official Guidebook to Becoming an Elite Cutman or Cutwoman. It will do for those who aspire to enter the world of boxing, Muay Thai or MMA as a professional cut person, what the *Boy Scout Handbook* does for scouts.

Adrian has demonstrated a history of working in the combats sports industry as well as the online media industry. He is a skilled teacher with experience in public relations, sponsorships, media management, website design and project management. Many in MMA know him as a coach.

Adrian is also the Founder and President of the *Fight Business Academy* in Las Vegas, Nevada. This organization provides formalized training for career opportunities in MMA, boxing and Muay Thai. It is a combination of an online Academy and live Boot Camps designed to prepare students for careers in elite-level fight promotions around the world. Adrian has established himself as a respected teacher and trainer in the elite world of fight promotion and management.

The sections in The Official Guidebook to Becoming an Elite Cutman or Cutwoman on how to learn and educate yourself are worth the price of the book alone. Adrian gets you on the right track early. You will learn basic and advanced skills as well as becoming knowledgeable about everything you need to be a professional such as visas, passports and using graphic designers and photographers to help build your career.

In my fight promotion experience since 1993, I have met few individuals who are as dedicated to fighter safety as Adrian Rosenbusch. Devour this book on becoming a cut person and you will be on your way to a new career.

## Foreword

*– Art Davie, Member of the UFC Hall of Fame & the Legends of MMA Hall of Fame.*

# THE TIME IS NOW!

"Human life is truly a short affair. It is better to live doing the things that you like. It is foolish to live within this dream of a world seeing unpleasantness and doing only things that you do not like."

— — Tsunetomo Yamamoto, Hagakure: *The Book of the Samurai*

*Adrian Rosenbusch and Swayze Valentine in Australia*

# 1
## WHAT IS A CUTMAN/CUTWOMAN?

First things first—what exactly is a Cutman/Cutwoman? We definitely need to begin by defining these terms. There is a lot of confusion about what exactly is a Cutman/Cutwoman since, until now, there has been no formal training on the subject. Infrequent seminars and extremely rare apprenticeships have been the only real way to access to any useful information. So let's change that and give these fighters the care they deserve. Deal? We're assuming you said "Yes" because you're here!

A Cutman/Cutwoman is a professional in the Combat Sports arena who has two main responsibilities. First, before the fight begins, Cutmen/Cutwomen wrap the fighter's hands with gauze and tape to prepare them for their fight. Second, during the fight, Cutman/ Cutwoman are responsible for attending to any damage to the fighter, or other issues within the scope of their practice, in less than sixty seconds in-between rounds.

Those are the two main parts of the job, but depending on the level of promotion, the particular Combat Sport, or situation, you could end up doing many more things. These might include helping the promoter or production crew with various tasks, getting food, organizing your hand wrapping schedule for the event, putting Thai Boxing liniment on a fighter's legs during a Muay Thai event, and much more.

We will cover the most likely scenarios you'll encounter in this profession, but just be aware that it is possible to be asked to do more. That being said, don't do anything that violates the regulations of the sanctioning body (such as an Athletic Commission) or that feels unethical. I have never been asked to do anything unethical by any well-known organization, so relax, it's not something you're constantly going to encounter.

Before we go any further, let's dispel a few myths about this line of work. The first myth is that Cutmen/Cutwomen actually pull out a surgical kit in-between rounds and suture cuts (stitch cuts shut) with a needle and thread. This is a frequently asked question and we'd like to clear that up. Sutures are done in a medical room at certain events by doctors in a completely sterile setting or in hospitals at other events. Sutures are delicate work that should only be done by a physician in the proper setting with no pressing time limits. As a Cutman/Cutwoman, this is definitely not in your scope of practice.

The second myth is that we actually cut fighters with a razor blade to relive the pressure from a hematoma (collection of blood underneath the skin) or swelling. Proper treatment for this is covered in the Fight Business Academy Online Course, but for now, just know that cutting someone would just add more damage to our equation and put the fighter in worse condition. Not to mention that the last thing you want around a fighter's eye is a razor blade. Yikes!

Third, is the most common question we get asked, "So are you a doctor or medic or something?" No, we're not doctors or medics or EMTs (Emergency Medical Technicians or Medics in some settings). I'm a Cutman. We completely understand why this is such an interesting question for people because of the medical nature of our work. Here is the truth, we are a crucial part of the medical team of any proper event and we have an extremely specialized skill-set that complements the rest of the fighter safety team.

The fighter safety team consists of Doctors, EMTs, Inspectors from a sanctioning body, and Cutmen/Cutwomen. We will go over the team in more detail later, but for now, just know that we are all crucial parts of this team. To further illustrate how different we are, it's important to understand that Fight Business Academy has trained Emergency Room physicians, surgeons, and paramedics to become Cutmen/Cutwomen. We have to train them because that's how different our area of expertise is. We all have our jobs to do and together we form a wonderful team that fully supports these fighters and keeps their safety as our shared priority.

So now that you've gotten an overview of the profession, here are some common scenarios of who Cutmen/Cutwomen work for and how.

The first scenario is an MMA (Mixed Martial Arts) event. For this event, we might be asked to show up on weigh-in day (the day before the fight) and have little or no duties that day—then the following day we preform all our duties. For these events, we are typically hired by the promoter to work with at least one other Cutman/Cutwoman to wrap the fighters' hands and have one Cutman/Cutwoman work the red corner and the other, the blue corner of each fight to make sure both fighters are cared for during the fight. The promoter, or someone from the organization responsible for payments, will be the one who pays the Cutman/Cutwoman.

The second scenario is working for a Muay Thai event. There is a very broad spectrum of scenarios for this particular Combat Sport. Sometimes we work for one fighter, or a team of fighters, or the whole event. We could start working with the fighter for a few weeks leading up to the fight, wrapping their hands for practice, or we could just show up on fight day and work one fight—it varies based on the particular situation you're in. You will be paid by whomever you are working for in your particular situation.

The third scenario is working a Boxing event. For Boxing, every fighter is responsible for hiring his or her own Cutman/Cutwoman and it is extremely typical to spend a much longer period of time with your fighter. You'll most likely wrap his or her hands for a good portion of the training camp (the weeks leading up to their fight). You'll also most likely assist the head coach with whatever he/she needs until after the fight is over. For this, you're paid directly by the fighter or his or her manager.

Ok, we've defined Cutmen/Cutwomen, dispelled a few common myths, and provided an overview of what the working arrangements are for the most popular Combat Sports. Now we can move on to the main part of this book, which is the roadmap that shows how someone who is extremely dedicated can get to where they are going.

# THE ESSENTIAL GUIDE TO BECOMING A CUTMAN/CUTWOMAN

The road to becoming an elite Cutman/Cutwoman must be one of humility, passion and commitment. It is important for you to understand that becoming an Elite Cutman/Cutwoman is strictly a path for a very self-motivated person who is both compassionate and sociable, and who loves learning. You will need to be deeply comfortable with yourself and be able to connect with strangers and make them feel at ease quickly. Connecting with people is a critical concept that is rarely discussed in this field, but it will make a tremendous difference in how well you succeed. This profession requires that you study very hard on your own and volunteer your time freely in order to gain knowledge and experience. If all of this sounds like the type of person that you are, then it makes sense for you to take the next step on this journey.

Not everyone wants to be an elite-level Cutman/Cutwoman. Some people want to help a friend or family member who's a fighter and can't afford to hire a Cutman/Cutwoman. Maybe you just want to support your gym's team or maybe you're a coach who has to do it all by yourself on fight day. Whatever your goal is, this guide can help you. By the way, all of the examples I just gave are from our students over the years, so as you can see, there are many reasons to get into this field. Goals can change, and that's something that keeps life interesting, so keep an open mind.

Now that we have the prerequisites covered, let's take a look at what the rest of the journey looks like. These are the steps you need to take in order to progress to the top levels of the sport.

## 2

## EDUCATION: WHAT TO STUDY TO GET RESULTS FAST

"An investment in knowledge pays the best interest."

— BENJAMIN FRANKLIN

The quality of your education in Combat Sports will determine your effectiveness for your entire career. If you are well trained, you will be able to provide superior care to athletes; if you are not, then you have already put a limit on your career. When the sanctioning bodies you work under see the quality of your education, including your competency, it will directly affect how far and how fast you will rise in the world of Combat Sports.

. . .

Find good sources of information to study so that you have references to draw from. Without good educational resources, you are just guessing and in Combat Sports that can be very dangerous.

To educate yourself you should:

- Study independently, on your own time, Cutman/Cutwoman specific skills with proper reference materials.

- Familiarize yourself with the regulations governing your local jurisdiction to start with, then familiarize yourself with a few other jurisdictions that you are interested in to see the differences.

- Study anatomy. The anatomy of the hand and head are the areas to focus on first, but as my mother always told me, "Education is never a negative." So study as many body parts as you can. Understanding the structures that you are working on will pay huge dividends in your career.

- Ask questions. You should ask well-thought-out questions when the time is appropriate. The quickest way to not get answers to your questions is to bombard working professionals with a stream of random questions. Keep your questions to the same person very limited. If you're at an event and you'd like to ask a question, first make sure the person you are asking isn't busy.

## 3

## LEARNING: WHAT YOU WERE NEVER TAUGHT IN SCHOOL

You might be asking, "Wait—didn't you just cover that?" No, learning is actually an entirely different subject than education, and one that's not necessarily covered in most educational experiences. This section on learning is critical for our evolution in any part of our life, not just as a Cutman/Cutwoman.

This entire section is dedicated to my parents, both of whom earned doctorates and were college professors. I was never a good student during my K-12 career; I daydreamed, wandered, and regularly bombed tests. I was assessed and it was determined that I had a learning disability. I was put into several remedial classes for the duration of high school and the bar was set lower for me, understandably. There was one teacher who took a look at all the evidence and suggested that I was actually brilliant and just unmotivated/uninterested in learning in a classroom. I remember telling him, "No I'm not brilliant. I'm actually just dumb." He laughed and showed me his findings. He said that I daydream because I was trying to find better ways to do things and that I didn't test well because I hadn't found ways to truly retain information. My point is that without finding an efficient way to connect with the material we want to absorb, we will always struggle to retain it.

Life has a sense of humor. One of the many lives I've led was that of a successful professional gambler, despite my worst learning disability being in mathematics. That's pretty ironic to say the least. In the end, it was about finding a meaningful way to connect with the subject matter.

**Types of Learners**

There are many different ways we can connect with our subject matter and truly bond with what we're studying. We all learn very differently and according to one theory, the VARK[3] model, it is suggested that there are four different types of learners.

. . .

<u>Visual Learners</u>: Need to see the relationships between ideas with their eyes to commit it to memory.

<u>Auditory Learners</u>: Need to hear information out loud in order to process it effectively.

<u>Reading/Writing Learners</u>: The process of reading, then writing down the information, has a more profound effect on long-term retention.

<u>Kinesthetic Learners</u>: Need to move and connect with the concept in a physical sense in order to bond with the concept completely.

If you take a look at these four types of learning, there is probably at least one that sounds more appealing to you. It might be that you have been learning in a way that is not optimal for your maximum long-term retention. Just keep experimenting with these strategies and you'll find the ones that serve you best.

**Strategies for Learning**

. . .

Here are some of my personal favorite strategies for learning. These are from a keynote I gave at the Warrior Retreat, hosted by Martial Arts Hall of Fame Inductee, Scott Bolan, in Las Vegas. Let's start with the gold standard of note taking—the Cornell Note-Taking System.

**The Cornell Note-Taking System**[5] is fantastic for listening to lectures or seminars. Professor Walter Pauk, who was an education professor at Cornell University in the 1950s, devised it. Professor Pauk released this information to the public in his best-selling book, "How to Study in College." For the Cornell Note-Taking System, you will divide a standard 8.5" x 11" sheet of paper into 3 sections. The first section is a standard note-taking area.

Note-Taking Section: Here you'll write notes that are as thorough as possible during the lecture without worrying about spelling, punctuation, or anything else. Just get as much information down as possible.

Cue Column: Leave this section empty during the lecture. After the lecture is over, this is where you'll refine your notes into the most useful information for that page. Keep these notes very short since you'll use them fully in the third section.

. . .

Summary: Using the information from your Cue Column, write out a few sentences that sum up what the page was about. Now you have a refined version of the raw notes that is much easier to use while you're studying.

Practice Test: The Practice Test is an effective way to follow up with your Cornell Notes. In practice testing you come up with your own questions and give yourself a test. This is a simple but very effective strategy.

For more information on how to review your Cornell notes, please see the link to the Cornell Note-Taking System in the "Sources" section at the end of the book.

**The Anatomy of Learning**

Forming new and more efficient neural pathways is the key to becoming good at anything.

Note: A physiological learning nugget for physiology/anatomy fans:[6]

New neural patterns are formed in the basal ganglia of the brain, which is a group of structures linked to the thalamus that are critical to habits and decision-making. A neural pattern or pathway is formed by a group of neurons that fire signals in a coordinated way that results in, for example, the coordinated contraction of a group of muscles.

Cells, with a white fatty substance called myelin, wrap around the axons that extend out at the end of neurons. Myelin acts as an insulator, preventing loss of signal as it moves down the axon. Myelination increases the speed and strength with which the signal reaches the end of the nerve. Physical training results in increased myelination of axons both in the brain and in the rest of the body. So basically, the more you practice, the more you prevent leakage of the signal in your nerves, and your responses become faster and more accurate and coordinated. Isn't that incredible?

The time needed for the process of forming these enhanced neural pathways is estimated to take from 30-90 days, according to different accounts. So the moral is that long-term change requires long-term commitment. You're actually changing the physiological structure of your brain when you form new habits. Very cool!

. . .

**Interesting Side Note:** Ancient Greeks and Romans distinguish between two types of memory: natural and artificial memory. Natural memory is intrinsic and instinctual; artificial memory is something that has to be trained and developed through learning and practice.

## 4
## MEANINGFUL PRACTICE FOR MAXIMUM RESULTS

**E**laborative Interrogation: This method is only recommended after you have developed a high level of proficiency in the subject matter. In this type of learning you are essentially playing the "why" game with yourself. As with any subject in the world, if you ask "why" after you identify the answer, you will rapidly get to a place of deep introspection.

**Memorization Techniques**, such as the following, are <u>not recommended</u> by Fight Business Academy. The stand we have taken on memorization is supported by the article, "Improving Students' Learning with Effective Learning Techniques: Promising Directions from Cognitive and Educational Psychology" by Dunlosky, J., et al. *Psychological Science Public Interest*, 2013, Vol. 14, Number 1, pages 4-58.

Highlighting: This is a very widely used and extremely ineffective method. Think about how well you've retained information by simply marking it in your study materials. There's no method to link this to deeper parts of your consciousness so it will stay at the most surface level possible.

Re-reading: Simply reading the section over again to try to make the material more familiar. This consistently yielded very low retention in studies.

Summarization: Condensing the body of information into an easier to digest section. Very low retention, but useful for multiple-choice tests where students do not have to access the information at a later date.

Keyword Mnemonic: Using what a word sounds like to create a memorable image in your mind. This method has been criticized as inefficient as well as having the potential to actually lead to accelerated loss of information due to confusion about which image relates to which keyword. **Note:** Despite the drawbacks, keyword mnemonics can be very useful for remembering vocabulary, particularly in a foreign language.

Use of Imagery: Visualizing text is useful for the memorization of text-based materials but it is limited to materials that are considered "image-friendly." At this time, Fight Business Academy concurs with the opinion of the aforementioned study that further research is needed to define the effectiveness of this method.

Rote Memorization: Saying the concept that you're trying to remember over and over out loud to try to commit it to memory. This method is widely regarded as the least likely method to result in retention. Fight Business Academy does not recommend rote memorization.

**Study Techniques** that have demonstrated that they yield moderate to high results are the following:

Practice Testing: Testing with low or zero risk involved to ascertain a current level of proficiency. This methodology yields consistently high results.

Distributed Practice: Studying a subject over time, as opposed to all at once. The inverse of this would be "cramming" for a test, which is often ineffective. Distributed practice also utilizes the leverage of a technique called "spaced repetition."

Spaced Repetition: "Spaced repetition leverages a memory phenomenon called the *spacing effect,* which describes how our brains learn more effectively when we space out our learning over time."— Thomas Frank, "How to Remember More of What You Learn with Spaced Repetition" https://collegeinfogeek.com/spaced-repetition-memory-technique[8]

Interleaving Practice: "Interleaving practice" has reported up to 43% more long-term retention when dealing with motor learning, which we use specifically during hand wrapping. Combining old and new material, and using different sections of material out of sequence can make our brain more flexible and will help us understand the material better. If we are forced to adapt to new situations, and not always arrive at the same destination or via the same path, we reach a much deeper understanding of the subject. S.C. Pan, 2015. "The Interleaving Effect: Mixing It Up Boosts Learning." *Scientific American.* https://www.scientificamerican.com/article/the-

Interleaving-effect-mixing-it-up-boosts-learning/https://effectiviology.com/

Interleaving/

Now onto Fight Business Academy's two most powerful keys to success in training world-class students: Visual Motor Rehearsal and Emotional Anchoring.

By itself, visualization has had mixed results in control groups because some in the control group would visualize even though they were instructed not to do so. Because of this, greater structure is needed in regards to "visual motor rehearsal."

**Visual Motor Rehearsal:** Dr. Denis Waitley introduced the practice of "visual motor rehearsal" from the Apollo program into the Olympic program as reported in the movie "The Secret" (2007).

*Using this program, Olympic athletes ran their event, but only in their mind. They visualized how they looked and felt when they were actually participating in their event. The athletes would then hook up to a sophisticated biofeedback machine. Its results told the real story about the value of visualization. The neurotransmitters that fired were the same that actually fired muscles in the same sequence as when they were actually running on the track. This proved that the mind cannot tell the difference between whether you're really doing something or whether it's just a visual practice. "If you've been there in the mind you'll go there in the body."*

– Dr. Denis Waitley, "The Secret," Directed by Drew Heriot. Written by Rhonda Byrne. Executive Producer, Paul Harrington. Prime Time Productions, 2007.

With results like these from NASA, as well as from Olympic Athletes, it is no wonder that Fight Business Academy has had such tremendous success using this strategy.

At Fight Business Academy, when we teach our students in a live setting, we tend to lean towards using emotional anchoring and visual motor rehearsal instead of pen and paper. When it comes to any part of the human interaction element of this line of work, these two elements have the greatest staying power. We've experienced superior results with these and we highly recommend them.

All of these different types of learning are available to you as you set up your study sessions. You can listen to the videos on *Fight Business Academy* in a car ride or read the PDFs as you watch the videos ... when you're not driving please!

The one area that you will need to find some familiarity with is the kinesthetic process. Putting your hands on tape and gauze and then molding them onto another human being is an area where touch will give you a tremendous amount of feedback. There is also an auditory component of listening to the tape rip and release from the roll that's an unmistakable signal of aptitude. When I go backstage at events I can literally hear who's an expert and who hasn't reached that level yet!

I recommend playing with these different types of learning to see which ones are yielding the best results for you, as well as, finding where and when your best studying is done. Generally speaking, when I'm learning something new, I like to watch videos on the subject I'm studying, first, then read about it to clarify the points I'm unsure of. Then I listen to the video again, to reinforce it while I'm doing other things, and, finally, I interact with the concept physically, if possible, to solidify the concepts. So find your best method and soak up all the information so that you have it when you need it.

## 5

# TRAINING WORLD CLASS STUDENTS

"Knowledge is of no use unless you put it into practice."

— Anton Chekhov

How much you practice by yourself on your own time will have a dramatic effect on how you perform—that is, provided that your practice is mindful and following a plan set forth by an expert. There are several things you can practice without being in front of the fighters you plan on assisting. The key is to make practice a daily ritual.

Daily practice is especially important in the beginning of your career. You need to build a strong foundation in order to be effective. You'll be using these skills every single time you step into a gym or an arena and you need disciplined repetition of them in order to add them to your long-term memory.

The way you practice will have a natural evolution, which makes perfect sense as you graduate each level. If you think about it, this is how you have mastered all the skills you have in your life, always building on the foundation you have just completed.

**Note:** Don't rush any of the phases! All stages of your development are critically important and need to be given their proper time. If you want to speed up your road to proficiency, the only way is to find a suitable mentor when you're ready. If you shortchange any of these phases, it will show at the most inconvenient and detrimental times, for example, when you are at an event and someone's counting on you.

Here are the phases that you'll notice when practicing:

1. <u>Beginner</u>: You are slow moving while looking directly at your training resource and you make frequent mistakes. This is totally fine! You should be in an open-book mode when you begin your journey—this shows that you are taking it seriously and want to take the time needed to really get your skills down. It shows

that you care about the people you intend to serve.
2. <u>Intermediate</u>: You are moving faster and only occasionally glancing at your reference materials to double check your work.
3. <u>Advanced</u>: This phase is where you start to really focus on achieving high-quality, consistently reproducible results. You also start thinking about the amount of time it takes you to complete any given task and really start focusing on reducing that time every day. At this stage, you're already producing really good work and you're feeling great.
4. <u>Mastery</u>: This level is ongoing. It will last you the rest of your career if you're mindful, and you should be thankful for that. The alternative is that you become arrogant or complacent, at which point you cease to evolve and you will eventually be left behind by someone who is more motivated than you are.

Mastery is when you no longer need to dwell on your protocols, but rather, how you feel and what your mindset is in the moment. With mastery, your focus will turn from external tasks to internal mindfulness. You will focus on centering yourself before working, you will focus on your breathing, and you will focus on the experience the person you're working on is receiving.

A very popular concept in achieving mastery is from author Malcolm Gladwell who, in his 2008 book "Outliers," proposed that it takes 10,000 hours of deliberate practice to become a master at anything. This concept was developed by Gladwell when he compiled case studies from a German violin prodigy all the way to Bill Gates.

Since then, there have been a few studies that have investigated these findings, and the results have been mixed. Note that the research team responsible for gathering the information for the book refutes the concept of 10,000 hours of practice being the magic key to mastery. Concerns such as these prompted Anders Ericsson, the lead researcher in Malcom Gladwell's studies, to further clarify several points in an interview with *Inc.* magazine.

---

> *"...Ericsson's research showed that it's not about hours of practice, it's about deliberate practice.... That's a kind of practice where you're not actually doing your job, you're actually taking time, where you're focusing in on trying to improve,"* Ericsson says. *"In particular, when you do that under the guidance of a master teacher, the teacher would be able to actually tell you what is going to be the next step here in your development. That is the kind of practice that we talked about as being essential to reach the highest level of performance."*

— ANDERS ERICCSON DURING AN INTERVIEW
WITH DAVID BURKUS, *INC.*, JUNE 7, 2016.

---

The point that made the most impact on us at Fight Business Academy is that practice needs to be deliberate and under the guidance of a master in the field that you are studying.

## 6

## VOLUNTEER TO BOOST YOUR SKILLS

Volunteering is the perfect way to gain extremely valuable real-world experience without too much pressure. The best way for Cutmen/Cutwomen to quickly get a feel for this career is to find a local gym in which to volunteer their time wrapping fighters' hands. This practice also acclimates you to the fight environment if you're new to the sport.

If you're already involved with Combat Sports and you're looking to add the expertise of being a Cutman/Cutwoman to what you're already doing, then this is also a chance to recalibrate your focus on an entirely different set of responsibilities. It's important that the people at the gym categorize you as someone who can provide them with additional help so that you stay on everyone's mind within the gym.

Here's the secret to getting maximum benefit from these sessions. Offer to wrap a fighter's hands before their class starts. The reason this is so beneficial is that there's a real-life time limit on your hand wraps. Training in this manner gets you used to the idea that there are penalties for not completing a task correctly and efficiently. If you don't wrap the fighters' hands properly, then they'll be uncomfortable during training and you'll most likely need to intervene quickly, which will irritate the fighter. If you don't wrap their hands quickly, then they'll be late to class, which interferes with their progress, which will cause them to be annoyed.

It is a luxury for a fighter to have his/her hands wrapped professionally with tape and gauze for a practice session, but only if it doesn't interfere with their training schedule. The fighter is at the gym to train and if you offer to wrap his/her hands, it will usually be a welcome invitation as long as they get the sense that you understand that they cannot be late for their class.

The goal is simple but the execution is difficult. Aim to wrap the fighter's hands quickly and professionally before their class begins. When you can accomplish this task you should be very proud of your progress. It is easy to overlook this important milestone in you career.

## 7

## A GREAT MENTOR IS KEY

> "One of the greatest values of mentors is the ability to see ahead what others cannot see and to help them navigate a course to their destination."
>
> — John C. Maxwell

Finding a good mentor is a critical step in your success. If you follow the wrong mentor, at best, you will have wasted your time and energy following someone who cannot help you reach your goals. At worst, a bad mentor will knowingly hold you back, drain your bank account, and work against you behind closed doors. No thank you!

. . .

A great mentor will make a dramatic difference in your education, as well as your career. Your mentor needs to be a perfect combination of knowledge, experience, availability to teach and ability to teach well.

In the previous "practice" section of this book, we heard researcher Anders Ericsson state that when you train under the guidance of a master teacher, that teacher should be able to tell you what is going to be the next step in your development. The master teacher he's describing is exactly what to look for in a mentor.

If you spend any time looking at successful people, you will notice that, more often than not, they all had a great mentor guiding them in their pursuit of greatness. Success is a team sport; you don't have to do it all alone.

Here's a quick list of questions to ask yourself about your mentor:

- Has my mentor been where I'm trying to go?

- Does my mentor give me a good vibe?

This is really important; you have to trust your gut.

- Is my mentor happy?

This is such an underrated question. If the person teaching you isn't excited about his/her own life, then why would you want him/her guiding you?

- Why would this person mentor you?

If they're at the top of their field then they're incredibly busy and most likely being asked frequently to mentor people. What you're getting out of the situation is obvious, but what would they gain? Every top person in a field thinks about one thing after they've spent some time at the top—their legacy. If you're able to frame for them how you would add to their legacy, then you've got a great shot.

## 8

## GET LICENSED

Licensing is a very important aspect for anyone in the field of Combat Sports, but many people are unsure of how to go about that process. Depending on where you are in the world, your licensing procedures may vary. As a general rule, you'll want to find your local jurisdiction, starting with a state-level jurisdiction. If that doesn't exist, then you will have to look for a national level commission. Some places only have the national level commission, but some also have state and/or tribal level jurisdiction.

The departments that handle licensing for Combat Sports can sometimes be housed in surprising entities. The way to find your state commission is to do an online search for MMA or Boxing licensing in your state/province/etc. Then, cross-reference that search with a "Seconds" license.

Officially, Cutmen/Cutwomen are listed as "Seconds" because the fighter is the primary in the ring and we are the secondary in the ring. You might also come across an amateur license option, which we also recommend acquiring. These licenses are typically valid for one year from the date of issuance, although some jurisdictions might also make the license valid for one calendar year, so make sure you know when your license expires.

The process for getting your license in most jurisdictions in the United States is very straightforward:

1. Find the information online about licensing.

2. Print out the license and fill it out.

3. Include 2 passport photos.

4. Include a check or money order for the appropriate fees. (Follow the payment instructions that are specified.)

5. Mail your packet.

Usually you will receive your license within two months, so please get your license **before** you have an event scheduled. Some events such as elite-level professional boxing might have a table on site to license people on the spot, but this is extremely rare, so don't count on it.

**Note:** Some jurisdictions want to make sure that applicants are not behind on any child support payments before they will grant you a license.

The optimal time to get licensed is as soon as you have started training. You never know when a friend or acquaintance might ask for your help at an event, and if you are already licensed, then you're ready to go! If it's an amateur event, a license to work the event may or may not be required. If you don't need one, then you are just extra prepared—which is always better.

In some jurisdictions, amateur licenses are available. In this case, we recommend getting both amateur and professional licenses. These are not available in many jurisdictions so if you can't find one, don't be surprised.

<u>International Jurisdictions</u>: Some jurisdictions in countries outside of the United States can require a substantial amount of paperwork in order to be licensed to work there. From the licensing, to the work visa required forms, you could be looking at quite an involved process. For more information about work visas see the "Visa" section of this book.

Getting a license isn't that difficult for most people, so that's not a major barrier to entry. But keeping one could be difficult if you don't know what you're doing. Your local sanctioning body has every right to revoke your license if you are violating the rules or you are a danger to the athletes.

# 9
# THE TRUTH ABOUT CERTIFICATION AND ASSOCIATIONS

Getting certified is an often-misunderstood subject because, to be honest, it's an emerging concept. Certification is not to be confused with licensing—they are separate issues altogether. Getting certified by a school means that you have satisfied their particular requirements for graduation. It may or may not mean that you are ready to actually start working, but it's a great first step.

If asked during a licensing application, sanctioning bodies will often look at a certification as a sign that you are taking the work seriously, which is fantastic. Any promises beyond that should be looked at with scrutiny.

. . .

There are a few amateur events that want you to pass through their in-house certification processes before allowing you to work for their larger events. This is entirely optional, and frankly not highly recommended at this point in time. You might be better off working several other amateur events and progressing toward professional events, depending on your personal goals.

As far as associations go, they should be viewed as "clubs" with no additional weight or importance being inferred. Even if some of the members are famous in the field, you should pause to ask what your involvement in that club includes. Typically, you pay a fee and you are sent a t-shirt with the club logo on it and you have your name and id number listed on their website. We have found no instances of fighters, promoters, or producers going to these websites to find qualified personnel. Getting hired is the responsibility of the individual. If joining a club still sounds fun, then by all means join one.

Note: At the time of publication, less than 15% of elite Cutmen/Cutwomen were part of any given association.

10

# WHY YOU NEED TO GET A PASSPORT NOW!

It might not seem necessary to have a passport now, but having one will open up the top levels of the field to you. Most likely, the opportunity to work abroad, for which you will need a passport, will happen in the blink of an eye, without any warning.

The day I realized that having a passport was critical was when I was cage-side during my UFC audition. One of the UFC executives was running into a problem where they weren't sure how they were going to take care of Cutmen for the first ever season of the Ultimate Fighter Brazil. The executive was considering all of her options, not sure exactly how they would handle it, when I interrupted, saying, "I'll live in Brazil for six weeks," which stopped her dead in her tracks. She asked me "do you have a passport?" I said "Yes!" and she said, "Do you have a passport now—as in can you go home right now and pick it up?" I said "Yes!" She replied, "Start packing your bags!" And that's how I got my first assignment with the UFC. Opportunity meets preparation!

Getting your passport as soon as possible should be very high on your list. Fight Business Academy has a great resource to assist with the process, which is one we have used professionally for years: cibtvisas.com/passports.

A new feature on CIBT is the digital photo service, which is amazingly helpful. On one of my previous passport renewals, before CIBT, I almost missed my anniversary trip with my wife because of an issue with the traditional photo process. I submitted all my information four months before my date of travel and nobody had any answers as to how to fix the problem. I had to drive to a passport agency a state away in order to get my passport squared away, and I still barely made my flight. For me, CIBT is the only way to do anything passports or visa related.

To use our CIBT widget and save 10% on your expedited passport services, please visit:

https://www.cibtvisas.com/?login=fightbusinessacademy

Fight Business Academy secured this partnership with CIBT to bring you this extremely valuable service. We sought out a partnership with CIBT because we've had such a long and reliable history with CIBT that we can recommend them without hesitation. (Please note that Fight Business Academy does receive a commission for every visa and passport service used through our link.)

### Pro Tip: Passport Replacement Coverage:

This is easily my favorite hidden gem in the passport world. For $40, at the time of print, CIBT offers passport replacement coverage. This means that CIBT will replace your passport and all your included visas should they be lost. They will, in fact, replace anything to do with your passport for up to $205 (at the time of publication)!

Seasoned international travelers instantly see the value in such a service. For those new to traveling internationally, getting a passport replaced in a hurry, let alone a visa, could have some devastating fees associated with it. This is all assuming you live in a state that has a passport center and that you can get an appointment at a passport center in time to make your flight. Of course, you would also have to get your visa, which would be a serious endeavor on a short timeline.

. . .

Instead of trying to do this alone, you would contact CIBT through an 800 number and they would get to work on their separate network to get you ready to travel. CIBT has a very large and efficient network to expedite passports and visas with a timeline that can save travelers from nightmare experiences—all for only a $40 add-on fee.

<u>Crazy True Story</u>: CIBT had a client that secured his passport about a week before he traveled and the delivery service left it on the front porch instead of having him sign for the package as should have happened. Right as it was delivered, a stray dog grabbed the package and ran down the street with it! The client heard the commotion and ran outside to find a dog chewing up his passport. This was a complete nightmare because he was traveling by the end of that week. He called CIBT, gave them his information, and he was on an international flight with his new passport in hand by the end of the week! This extreme situation was all handled by his $40 passport replacement service. That true story shows an extreme version of how valuable this service is. They need to film that as a commercial in my opinion because—wow!

# 11
## VISAS

Visas are another subject that goes hand-in-hand with passports. Depending on your country of origin and the details of your visit, you might also need a visa to work a gig in another country. The length of time and paperwork required to get a visa depends on the country you're visiting. Some visa applications might require letters of reference and a work related resume, so it's important to get an official itinerary of your journey so that you have the dates and locations of all the shows for your trip.

Elite-level promotions may have an in-house department to help you with your visas, but it's better to familiarize yourself with the process from the beginning. Getting a visa can be a daunting process, but with time and experience, it becomes less so.

It is your responsibility to research whether or not you need a visa to work in another country, but Fight Business Academy can help with that. To see whether or not you will need a visa for a particular country, please use our CIBT widget by visiting: https://www.cibtvisas.com/?login=fightbusinessacademy

## 12

## AMATEUR EVENTS

Taking part in amateur events is not for just a short period of time, nor is it something to be eager to finish up with quickly. Amateur events are a great opportunity to apply all of the knowledge that you've gained and to make a few mistakes—as we all do when we are learning something new. That's right—you need to make the majority of your mistakes here. The more complete your education is, the fewer mistakes you'll make, but mistakes are inevitable. If you have a knowledgeable and invested mentor, he/she will be able to catch many potential mistakes before they're ever made on the job. Learn from your mistakes and don't make the same ones twice, then you're on the right path.

This is the time when you'll experience the most rapid growth in your career. We always keep learning, but the lessons will come at a more rapid fire pace in this phase.

There will be a lot of information to process after every event you work, so it's good to make time to jot down notes so that you can refer to them later.

Amateur events are where you'll make an abundance of important contacts. Many of the people you meet at amateur events will be people who are around you all the way into a professional career. The inspectors, coaches, photographers, doctors, and many others will be present during professional events.

From the first amateur event you work, you should get used to the idea of creating and updating checklists. Make a checklist of all the equipment you need to bring, what you need to resupply after each event, etc. Personally, I'm notoriously bad at packing; the only thing that makes me show up ready to work without any worries are my checklists. This is amplified when you travel internationally, when whatever you have in your bags, is the only thing you'll have on fight night.

## 13

## VOLUNTEERING VS. GETTING PAID

This is another important topic to address because there is no clear time when you should make this transition.

We often get questions about when it's appropriate to volunteer your services and when you should start to charge for them. The answer is up to you, but we recommend volunteering for your first promotion in every Combat Sport at the amateur level. Remember to limit the total number of events that you volunteer for, because once a promoter is used to having your services for free, you'll be hard pressed to convince them to pay you later on.

Volunteering for amateur events is a great idea to build up your skillset and network. That being said, once you develop your network a little more, you can ask if others have been paid for working as a Cutman/Cutwoman for that event. Then you can formulate your pitch based on that information.

Volunteer for charity fight events, if you can, since this is a great way to put some positive energy behind your efforts and meet like-minded people. An intermediate strategy can be to ask for a stipend for your material costs of working the event, that way it's not costing you money to gain valuable experience.

There are also pro-am events that feature both professional and amateur bouts on the same card. These are fantastic transitional events for you. Unfortunately, they're not extremely common so if you find one, jump at that opportunity. At this level, you should be starting to charge the promoter for your services.

Amateur events can potentially be either a free or paid event depending on the level of the promoter, but Pro-Am should definitely be a paid gig. From Pro-Am and up, the promotion is paying athletes, so they need to pay you for your time spent taking care of them.

## 14

## NETWORKING

Networking is a vital part of your career. Your ability to effectively connect with others in the industry will open up more opportunities that you can imagine. When people like you, they'll open up doors for you; when they don't like you, they won't. In this industry, huge decisions are usually made behind closed doors and people's impressions of you are what seal the deal. So, if you're leaving a good impression on as many people as possible, then you're in a good spot.

One misconception about networking is that it is a surface interaction that's a contrived attempt to better your status. Great networking is about creating a feeling of community in which you find people that you truly enjoy and, together, you find ways to facilitate mutual success.

Spend some money on a professional business card, and remember that it is a representation of who you are, that's for starters. Now that you have your awesome business cards, don't just try to hand out as many as you can, instead, look for quality interactions, not quantity. Start genuine dialogues with the people around you at gyms or events. Don't be embarrassed about what part of your journey you're on—everybody started somewhere.

**Note:** This tip was given to me by the former General Manager of Team Quest MMA, Scott McKendry.

**Showing genuine interest in other people first, will lead them to want to find out more about you.**

This point seems very logical, but when you are networking, it can sometimes slip your mind as you try to introduce yourself, individually, to a room full of people.

When you are networking be sure to:

- Have well-designed, professional business cards on hand;

- Have an updated work resume ready; (Note: This

is usually only used for elite-level promotions and international events.)

- Research the people who you want to meet and be ready to talk about their latest event;

- Show up well-fed, well groomed, well rested, and well informed;

- Make sure you've watched all the latest Combat Sports events, not just the ones in your sport.

**Tip:** For every person you meet, write their name down along with a one-sentence descriptor of what they look like and who they are. I do this on my phone as soon as I walk away from an interaction. The next time you run into this person, greet him/her by name in a friendly and familiar manner. This is the first step in building rapport.

## 15

## BUILDING REAL RAPPORT

This is one item that can stop people, who are very knowledgeable and otherwise fantastic candidates, from moving forward in the field. The truth is, if people don't associate your performance with your name, you will struggle. Also, if you don't leave people with a positive impression of yourself, then it's hard to build a good reputation.

You want people to add to the positive impression they have of you from the last time they saw you. This is what will assure that when an opportunity arises with someone you've met, your name is at the forefront of their mind as someone they would enjoy working with or be confident in referring to others. People recommend people they like and that they know can get the job done right. It's simple.

Humility plays a big part in your long-term success or failure. If people see that you are humble and sincere, they will want to work with you.

The two most overlooked groups with which to build rapport are:

<u>The Photographers covering the events that you're working</u>: We'll cover the subject of photographers more in a bit, but for now, just think about this: along with the video crew, these are the men and women who capture the essence of an event forever. These people are framing the most impactful moments of any given event—and you'd like them to consider including you in those photos. If that's the case, you should definitely get to know them.

<u>Your local Athletic Commission and other sanctioning bodies</u>: These are the people who you will work with from your first amateur event all the way through your professional events. When they get to know and like you, as well as when they recognize your high level of training, they will be an asset to you. When you're getting to bigger and bigger events, the Commission will already be comfortable with you, which will put the Promotion at ease.

. . .

<u>Case Study</u>: During my UFC audition, the Athletic Commission made it ten times easier to make a good impression. As I walked into a locker room to wrap a fighter's hands, one of the Inspectors I had built rapport with greeted me warmly and made a friendly comment about me being the best, which raised some eyebrows in the best possible way. That audition felt like I had a home court advantage because familiar faces, on which I had already made a great impression, surrounded me.

## 16

## WORKING WITH FAMOUS PEOPLE

As you rise on your journey into the profession, you'll run into people who are your heroes, or, at least, who are very famous. It's important to be mindful of their armor-plated skin and their ability to breathe fire . . . just kidding! More often than not they're very down-to-earth people who happen to have very cool jobs. This relates to your work in the fight industry because you'll most likely come into contact with celebrities outside the ring/cage, as well as working for famous athletes.

More often than not, when you meet a famous person, they first just want to make sure that you're not going to do anything crazy around them. Then, when they see that you're normal enough, they'll relax quite a bit. Celebrities constantly have to be extra aware of how people are behaving around them because fans are known to do highly irregular things in the presence of their idols.

When meeting these famous people, not losing your cool around them can take some mindfulness. Please be sure not to base your opinions of the famous people you meet based on their media coverage, especially fighters. I've lost track of how many people outside of the industry have told me that they "hate" a certain fighter, but once I've given them some real-world examples of how that fighter behaves when they're not trying to hype a fight, they sit back and re-evaluate. You might become the favorite Cutperson of a super-famous fighter that has a villain persona on camera but in real-life they're kind and appreciative of your services.

Question your preconceived notions about celebrities and prepare to be pleasantly surprised by which ones are the most fun in person. There are a few famous fighters who are not ideal to work with—but they are definitely the exception. Most fighters will be very appreciative of you as an elite Cutperson and will know that you are looking out for their safety. I can assure you, the majority of your interactions with famous fighters will be positive and interesting.

. . .

**Awesome Case Study:** My mother is a retired college professor and one of the sweetest persons on the planet. One day she told me that she met the most interesting man on a flight who said he was a boxer. They were sitting next to each other in First-Class for a 4-hour flight, and during the flight he was telling her stories about what being a Boxer was like. My mother, being such a classic mom, showed him pictures of me and told him about my love of Martial Arts. He thought it was particularly fascinating that I was so appreciative of the Samurai culture. He was stunningly well read about the Samurai, Japanese culture, famous philosophers, and history in general. My mom, being a very intelligent college professor, could speak at great lengths about those subjects also. The two of them had a fantastic flight and my mother described him as "a very humble and intelligent young man."

She was trying to remember his name, so I looked up famous boxers on Google because I was so curious as to which one it could be. Then I had a feeling that life was about to really amuse me and I typed in one last name... "Oh yes, that's him!" exclaimed my mother. The boxer she had spent a fascinating flight with was Mike Tyson!!! I laughed so hard that such an intimidating and iconic boxer was my sweet mother's travel buddy! So Mr. Tyson, if you are reading this, my mom thinks you're awesome and you'll never be dethroned as her favorite boxer. Thank you for being so kind to my mother.


Even people who were described as a "natural" or "prodigy" weren't as amazing when they started, as they are now. They were probably pretty bad, but they stuck with it and put some discipline behind their talent, and that's why they are now superstars. What is the point of all this? You have the right to learn and grow!

## 17
## SOCIAL MEDIA: A QUICK AUDIT

Social media is a fact of life now for almost 3 billion users, according to recent studies. That means that almost everybody you're going to work with in your career will have a social media account. So what does that mean in the world of professional Combat Sports? It means that people will be able to find your social media profile just from a cursory Internet search—so it's important to think about what your profile looks like to your career.

Social media is a relatively new technology that is shaping the way human beings interact with the world around them. Our public social media profiles tell the world so much about who we are as a person and what we value.

The one thing most people don't fully appreciate is that anyone is able to find our social media profiles and extract information from them. No, this isn't a tangent about online privacy and "big brother"—instead it's an invitation to look at your social media profile from the eyes of a potential employer in the fight business.

I have seen firsthand how people can lose out on major opportunities because they do not govern themselves properly on social media. I've seen people be fired from the jobs that they had because they posted something that shouldn't be online. Please take a moment to look at your own profile from an objective viewpoint. Think about it—how many celebrities have gotten themselves into a bad situation because of a post they made on social media? Also remember that these major celebrities have a public relations team to assist them whenever they get into a bad spot. So ask yourself, do you look like someone that promoters should trust with the safety of their fighters? This is not to say that your social media profile should be a sterile resume with no photos, but just keep it appropriate.

So for our quick audit, let's look at your situation from the eyes of the promoter.

<u>Things that generally won't work in your favor on Social Media:</u>

- Pictures you wouldn't want them to see. Are there photos of heavy drinking, drug use, lewd

behavior, etc.? If so, these might make you look like a liability—or at least unreliable.
- Offensive posts about religion or politics. Are there photos in which you are insulting someone with opposite beliefs? These might make you look difficult to work with. Promoters don't need any drama.
- Posts showing clear favoritism for one fighter over another? Promoters want an unbiased professional, not a fan.
- Posts complaining about work, co-workers, or your boss?

Things that do work in your favor:

- Photos of you wrapping hands and working events.
- Photos of you enjoying life.
- Sharing positive news: family events, heartwarming stories, motivational posts—almost anything, as long as it's positive. People like to work with happy people—it's simple.

## SECRET WEAPON: PHOTOGRAPHER

Photo credit Joe Piccirillo / Joe Pic Photography

The next two sections focus on two completely unsung heroes who are worth their weight in gold. You need to find people who are not only skillful, but who you like to work with and who always deliver on time and on budget. These people will capture your incredible moments and then turn them into informational art that lets the world see the quality of your work.

For me, working with a good photographer was one of the most underrated keys to success in Combat Sports. Photographers are connected beyond belief in the community and able to mingle with every single facet of the sport enthusiastically. Photographers can facilitate so much more than you would ever imagine. The photographer who helped launch my career was Joe Piccirillo, aka, Joe Pic.

Case Study: To demonstrate just how powerful the right photographer can be, I'll tell you how I met Joe Pic. I found an amateur MMA event that I wanted to work and I saw that they were having a Ring Girl competition at a nightclub on the strip in Vegas. I knew this was a golden opportunity to network with the promoter and the crew because they were having a good time and they didn't have a promotion to run that night. I got ready to go out and showed up at the event with my cellphone to take some pictures with people while introducing myself to them at the same time.

It was failing miserably, which I noticed very quickly, so I decided a change in tactics was in order to salvage the night. I ordered a drink and hung back and watched who was working the room. I saw that there was one person that everyone was happy to talk to—and it was one of the photographers. He had rapport with everyone. They all wanted their picture taken by him, and he had a fantastic energy to him.

I waited until he stopped to check the setting on his camera and I approached him. I introduced myself and asked him if he was getting paid to work the event. He said "Yes," and I asked him if he'd like to make an extra $75 to introduce me to people in the room and take our picture together for my Website. He looked at me a little puzzled while he thought it over and then said "Okay, let's do this!"

The night took off like I was shot out of a cannon and I met so many people I almost lost track! Joe Pic was the only factor that turned what was a dead-end night into a wild success.

I worked that amateur MMA event for over a year while I made contacts and grew my skillset to the point where I was constantly working and getting bigger events all the time. Joe and I continued to work together for the rest of my career and his photographs helped launch my website and promotional materials into the stratosphere. That is why I can't stress enough the importance of a great photographer.

## 19

## SECRET WEAPON: GRAPHIC DESIGNER

Graphic designers are another group of people who can really make you shine. Like photographers, great graphic designers are well-connected people who know about events and emerging concepts before the general public. A great graphic designer can help you design a quality aesthetic for your business cards and website that will act as a 24-hour representation of who you are to the outside world. Because of this, it's worth your time to get it right. Unlike photographers, it may or may not be a good idea to hire graphic designers that you meet at local events. This depends greatly on where you live. Above all, make sure that you're able to review the websites of people that you're considering hiring. If you don't like the flow of the websites they build, or if you think the look isn't appealing, then you don't need to go any further with them.

## Website

As a former executive for a social media company, I can speak volumes about what makes a good website—but here are the key points to focus on:

User Interface: A user interface refers to how you're able to navigate the website to find the information you're looking for. Think about favorite websites you like to visit. How are they arranged? How easy is it to know where to go to find the information you want?

Aesthetic: This one is the main reason why people click away from a website that might have great information. If the site is not pleasing to the eye, then why would anyone want to hang out there? This is a huge representation of who you are, so make sure this accurately reflects the quality of who you are to the industry. It's got to have good curb appeal!

Updates: Once the website is completed, with all the photographs and content by the graphic designer, then how do new updates get added? If the designer offers to add new photos for you, that's not going to cut it. You need to be able to go into the back end of your site and add new photo galleries and new blog posts 100% on your own. There are several platforms that are very user-friendly and easy to update. The most commonly used platform is *Wordpress*, but there are several other platforms that you might feel comfortable using, so try some demos online. You can hire freelance graphic designers on site such as *Fiverr* and *Upwork* to help you customize these existing platforms so that they work well for you.

Hosting: You should own your own hosting solution for your website. Just ask your designer what size of hosting you'll need for your site. Most likely you'll be using "shared hosting" in which you'll share server space with other websites. This is a budget-friendly option that will be more than enough, unless you decide to make a very elaborate website or if you expect more than a few thousand people a day. You can always upgrade later on.

Domain: Make sure that you buy your domain name personally—don't have anyone do it for you. Sometimes you can get a fantastic deal by buying multiple years up front, but that's up to you. Purchasing your domain name through the company you want to have host your site can yield some very beneficial results later on—so keep that in mind.

SSL: SSL certificates are great add-ons to your website to secure the connection and the data being transmitted. A basic SSL certificate can cost about $75 per year and is fairly simple to connect to your website. More complex SSL certificates can be more difficult to connect to your website and are more expensive.

Support: When something unexpected happens to your website who is going to be assisting you? There can be a very wide variety of things that can come up with even the most user-friendly platforms. It's important to know who will be helping you. It might be a combination of the designer and the company who's hosting the site for you. You definitely want to know this sooner rather than later.

<u>Email</u>: There are free email accounts such as Gmail and Yahoo that are very reliable options and there are paid email accounts that will give you the "@yourwebsitename" address that connects to your domain. Please make sure that you feel comfortable using whichever email account you decide to go with.

<u>Pricing</u>: The price tag that goes with your website can have a huge range. A nice Wordpress site can range from $500-$20,000 depending on who's building it.

<u>Do-It-Yourself</u>: Another option can be a "do-it-yourself" type of service where you would pay a monthly rate and use templates to put your site together. This is a popular option because you can still hire freelance graphic designers to modify the templates and add widgets to give it a custom look.

## Business Cards

Every once in a while someone will tell you that the idea of a business card is outdated. Yet in almost all business situations people will still ask you for a card. There are many excellent and creative techie ways to stay in contact with people, but a business card has remained constant.

This is an area where you need to be mindful of the experience someone will have when you hand him or her your card. If you get print-at-home cards, the quality will demonstrate that you don't offer value. This is a perceived notion, but it's one that will help craft the person's impression of you. In this industry, there are only a few resources someone can use to get an impression of who you are. A business card is a physical representation of your brand and your value.

Take the time to have a good graphic designer design your cards. Then have your cards professionally printed on a premium card stock or other premium material. There are cards make of plastic, metal, wood, and even silk! Simply put, premium cards look and feel professional. The tactile impression of the card seems like a silly up-sell to those who aren't keeping track of people's reactions when they hand them a nice card. If it feels nice to the touch, then that translates as another area of perceived value.

Ultimately, you need to decide which type of card represents you the best, so make sure the lasting impression you make is a positive one.

## 20

# FIRST PRO EVENT: HOW TO MAKE IT A LAUNCHPAD, NOT A CEILING

---

"Be an asset, not a liability"

— SHEEPDOG RESPONSE

---

Getting your first professional event is a major, measurable step in your career. To get here, you've had to develop a superior skill-set along with very meticulous networking, along with building rapport. Be sure to thank whoever facilitated this opportunity—this is important because without gratitude, your world will get smaller and smaller.

If you met the promoter, and they hired you directly, make sure to follow up with them after the event via email and thank them for the opportunity. Let them know you're eager to help the promotion on their next event. Follow-up is an extremely underrated practice that cements your quality in a promoter's eyes—so don't neglect it. Calling or texting can be overwhelming to a promoter, and they have their plates full, so stick to email unless they ask you to do otherwise. Don't expect a response immediately, because they're exhausted after an event.

If you've put in some serious time at gyms and events and studied very hard, this should be a wonderful experience —although a little nerve-racking—but that's a very normal and healthy feeling. If you're nervous, that means you're treating this moment with the respect it deserves, and that's exactly the attitude you should have. Be confident and acknowledge that this is just the leap you need to make in order to grow.

Share the event on social media. Promoting the event yourself is always appreciated, just make sure to keep it positive and neutral. Don't take sides on fights, especially publicly—it won't benefit you. You can talk about how great the matchups are, or what a great event it is, and also share any ticket discount codes the promotion is offering.

Before you go to your first pro event, make sure that you're comfortable getting to the venue and be sure that you get there early. In ten years as an active Cutman, I've never had a promoter be anything less than happy that I was there ahead of the scheduled time. On the other hand, I've seen Cutmen stroll in 10-20 minutes late and never work that show again.

Another benefit to showing up early is that you can exchange business cards with the cage-side photographers so that you can find out where shots of you working the event will appear.

Make sure you get as many of the people's names as possible when you're working the event. Remembering these names will make that night go much better and breed some instant familiarity.

If there's a problem at the event, don't complain about it, instead, find a solution and help the show move forward.

. . .

In general, you should find ways to be helpful while not neglecting your job duties. Be an asset to the promotion every time they work with you and you'll quickly garner their respect.

Most people you interact with will treat you as a member of the production, so think about how well you're representing the promotion. You must be kind, efficient, professional, personable, flexible, in control of your task at hand, and very well informed about everything going on that night.

On event night you need to be:

- Well-rested,
- Well-prepared,
- Well-groomed,
- Well-fed,
- In a genuinely happy and helpful mood,
- In a good headspace.

Headspace is critical at events. You need to develop some fight-night rituals to get you in a good headspace. Find what series of pre-fight activities put you in a happy and confident headspace. Maybe listening to some music gets you in a great mood, eating at a certain time, watching a video or movie, or anything that helps. I would advise not directly involving anyone else in your ritual because that becomes an unpredictable element.

Only have rituals that you control. Favorite foods are fine in the beginning, but once you start traveling, then that ritual becomes difficult and stressful instead of fun.

My personal rituals:

- Set alarms on my phone for every activity I want to do;
- Triple check all my gear with my checklist;
- Eat something good at least an hour before I leave and make sure I'll be able to eat well when I'm done. (When traveling, I'll order extra food and put it in the fridge at the hotel for later);
- Watch movies while I get ready;
- Remind myself how much work I've done to get to the event I'll be at;
- Think about how many people I will get to be kind to tonight;
- Remind myself that, no matter what unexpected thing happens that night, I will handle it like a professional;

- Remind myself to enjoy this moment and be thankful for it.

Whatever your ritual is, make sure that at the end of it you feel:

Powerful,

Happy,

Confident,

Excited to get to work.

If you have all of these things and all of the gear you need, you'll be in good shape to tackle this milestone.

**Tip:** The night before your event, look at the fight card and familiarize yourself with what all the fighters look like. Go to the weigh-ins so that you see all the fighters and introduce yourself to the promotion when they're not busy. This will make it much easier to locate them once you're on site and on the show schedule. It's also a great idea to offer to assist in any way possible during the weigh-ins—that is you adding value that will build a relationship. This takes some extra effort, but it really pays off when you need it.

## 21

## SPONSORSHIP

Sponsorship is the most reliable method of making a financial difference in your career as a Cutman/Cutwoman. I've been very fortunate to discover ways to maximize my sponsorship opportunities during my career. My success with sponsorships has been one of the top reasons other elite-level professionals contact me. I'm happy to share my experiences here in hopes that you can have the same success.

I've had sponsors from a very early point in my career and, while it was definitely a learning process, the benefits far outweighed any negatives. I have seen so many people who lack an understanding of what makes a good sponsorship arrangement that I knew it was an important topic to include in this book.

The sponsorship that really put me in the spotlight was when I negotiated a contract to receive stock options in a company every time I appeared on TV. That deal definitely caught the attention of my peers. The company received the media exposure they wanted from the logos on my vest and I was directly invested in the company. It was a win-win

**Defining Sponsorship**

I am not going to copy and paste the dictionary definition of sponsorship because that won't help us here. Instead, let me define it in a way that really paints an accurate picture. Sponsorship is a relationship—plain and simple. You need to view the process of getting someone to give you something in return for you wearing their logo as a relationship that's beneficial to you.

A mercenary mindset is only going to lead to one-off deals or very short-lived business opportunities. What you really want is to have long-term relationships that you value. You need to find a sponsor that is a good match and let that sponsor know that you appreciate them and their product—not just the financial benefits of being associated with them.

**The Cringe-worthy Status Quo**

The most common, and cringe-inducing, approach to getting a sponsor is the version I see on social media from someone with a mercenary mindset, for example:

*"I've got a fight coming up! For fight shorts logo sponsorship opportunities, hit me up!"*

Nope. If you do the exact opposite of that real-world example in every way, then you're on the right track. Let's break down exactly what's wrong with this approach.

1. It's incredibly lazy! Sponsors are looking for someone who is motivated and interested in actively promoting their brand.
2. All you're offering is a logo placement on your shorts, which is not very committed. Are you planning on doing anything else? Social media shout outs? Anything else?
3. Apparently you don't care who the sponsor is, so how could they reasonably expect you to effectively promote their brand?
4. The sponsor has to approach you?! You can't be bothered to reach out to them? As if a great sponsor is actively searching for you on social media just hoping to give you a portion of their hard-earned promotional budget. Great sponsors are not going to respond to half-hearted attempts like that.

## Sponsorship Types and Levels for Cutmen/Cutwomen

Sponsorships for Cutmen and Cutwomen come in a huge variety of forms—which is another reason they are so exciting. But for the purposes of this section, we'll separate them into the three most common types of sponsorships and into three levels of sponsorships. It's possible that you will encounter a combination of these sponsorship types as you continue on your journey, so stay flexible in your thinking.

**Types of Sponsorships:**

<u>Discount</u>: In a discount sponsorship arrangement, you would negotiate a significant discount on the sponsor's product for yourself in exchange for your promotion of their brand. First things first, look at what supplies you are using in order to keep working events. Any product that gets used up and needs to be replaced should be your first priority. A great example would be an athletic tape sponsor, where you know that you'll be using the sponsors' product every time you step out the door to work. A "discount" or "product" sponsorship for tape would be extremely helpful.

The easiest way to go about arranging a sponsorship is to research whether the company offers "Pro Deals." Many companies, for example, offer steep discounts (typically 30-40%) to people who fit certain criteria. These are either employees or professionals working in the field who use their products as part of their profession.

If this deal goes through, the easiest way to execute the discount is to have the company generate a "discount code" exclusively for you that you can use to shop on their website. (They can even link this code to your IP address if they like.) That way you don't need to bother them every time you need something. This makes it super-easy for everyone involved.

This type of sponsorship is perfect for people getting started in their career. This is a small "ask" and it gives both parties plenty of room to grow together. Negotiating this type of deal also will be much less intimidating for you the first time around, which is an added bonus.

**Product:** Product sponsorships take the next logical step up from the "discount" sponsorship. You receive the sponsor's product for free in exchange for a more involved promotional schedule. You can clearly gauge that you've developed a great relationship with your sponsor when they are willing to move to the next level with you. That being said, there is no reason you can't approach a company with this type of offer right off the bat. It's all in what you are able to negotiate and how much the company sees a benefit in working with you. This type of sponsorship is more typical when you have established yourself in the field or, at least, you are easily recognizable in your local circuit.

**Pro Tip #1:** One reason you should feel confident about this type of sponsorship is that, especially with larger companies, people would rather give you free products or services than money. I've received incredible perks from international brands early on in my sponsorship history. These perks seemed like they were not a big deal at all to the company, but they were incredible to me. These perks included cases of brand new products and fully catered multi-day events!

**Paid:** This is the type of agreement that everybody thinks of when they think of a sponsorship deal. Paid sponsorships take a lot of preparation to be able to arrange. You need to know the company inside and out, as well as being able to articulate exactly how your arrangement will benefit the company.

You want to pitch yourself to the sponsor as a "Brand Ambassador." This shows that you know their product and that you believe in them strongly enough to put your name on their company roster. This is an opportunity for the sponsor to have a respected expert in the Combat Sports community deliver talking points directly to potential customers in a very natural way. People will ask you about the sponsors on your jacket and you will have talking points ready to go. Just make sure that they don't sound artificial, or people will view the interaction as inauthentic and lose interest.

**Pro Tip #2:** Do not try to "Wow" the sponsor by promising them an uptick in sales because of your involvement. First of all, it's difficult to equate your appearance at a show with a specific number of sales and secondly, it's unlikely you'll be able to deliver on that. Most sponsors I've met with would see that as a very amateur tactic because anyone experienced in asking for sponsorship would avoid promising that. Instead, you can use points like "establishing more brand recognition" at that particular event or "developing brand loyalty" or whatever the sponsor's prime objective is.

This is the time to know what kind of marketing objectives the sponsor has and why sponsoring you is the best use of those funds. Be sure to have all of your personal marketing items in place before you approach a sponsor for this type of opportunity. Also, don't expect a "one phone call close" with this type of sponsorship. This is an important decision for the sponsor and they'll probably want to negotiate with you on it.

**Pro Tip #3:** With any type of sponsorship you can always add an affiliate component to the deal. By "affiliate component" I mean that you can ask the company to provide you with an affiliate link to promote. If you've never heard of an "affiliate link," here's all that you need to get started. An affiliate link is a custom website link that tracks who clicked on the link and credits the person who it was created for if a purchase is made. This is an extremely popular form of "passive income" which is potentially a very helpful way of increasing your earning power.

Your affiliate link works like this:

1. You and the sponsor agree to the terms of the link i.e. how much commission you receive and what kind of discount you can offer with your link ("save 20% on your order with this link").

2. The sponsor issues you your custom-tracking link.

3. Share the link on your social media pages, forums, newsletters, blog posts, YouTube videos, and anywhere else you're actively promoting yourself. Don't spam people with unsolicited emails or the company will be unhappy with your promoting efforts.

4. Get paid!

The affiliate link is a nice add-on because it shows the company that you're willing to earn their sponsorship from Day 1. Even with a "discount" sponsorship, this is an excellent add-on. Not all businesses are set up for affiliate marketing programs, but it's always a good item to bring to the table.

**Levels of Sponsorship:**

**Local:** As the name suggests, these sponsors are in your hometown and are usually small businesses. These types of sponsors are used to small sponsorship proposals from local sports teams and amateur groups so they might be more receptive to events in their area.

**Professional:** These sponsors are more recognizable brands that will have plenty of room to grow with you as you continue in your journey. These sponsors have the ability to make a large difference in your career.

**Elite:** Brands that are household names or have huge financial opportunities attached to them. Landing one of these sponsors is definitely a game-changer for anyone.

**How to Pick which Sponsors to Approach?**

Make a list of the companies whose product you already use, that's the most genuine and straightforward approach. You already appreciate their products and agree with their messaging so that's the perfect place to start.

Next, make a list of companies whose products or services you'd like to have. Some of these products might be luxuries, like nice watches, for example (a very popular choice for Cutmen/ Cutwomen). These companies will usually appreciate that you're a fan of theirs, which is a nice place to start a relationship.

Take a look at the events you're going to be working and see who's sponsoring them. Also, it's important to research which brands have been actively promoting themselves at other events in your area. They are clearly trying to promote their brand, so give them a new exciting option.

**Research the Sponsors:** Does the company have a "sponsor" section? If so, you should make sure to read it and make sure that you submit your proposal in their desired format. Some companies receive large volumes of proposals so they need everything submitted in a uniform fashion that will make it easy to compare offers.

Read the company "About Us" page. This is a very important step because the sponsor can, and should, ask you why you're interested in them. If you don't have a good answer, it shows you're only interested in money.

What's the latest news about them? Google them and check out their social media.

Ask yourself if you and the sponsor are a good match. You will find, after you've done a little research about them, that there are some sponsors that wouldn't be a good fit for you. That's a good thing. You want this to be a partnership that is founded on common beliefs. Make sure they fit your personality. If they are a very proper company and you are a little edgy, then that might be a bad fit.

**Get Creative: Unusual Sponsors**

In combat sports there are sponsors that everyone wants a deal with—such as clothing brands, which can be terrific sponsors—but there's more out there to be explored. Many potential sponsors rarely get approached because most Cutmen/Cutwomen concentrate their efforts on the same things: combat sports clothing, combat sports athletic equipment, watches, and tape.

Don't get me wrong, these are all great sponsor to have, but you might find a goldmine just one or two steps off the beaten path. Don't be afraid to approach some sponsors that you like that your colleagues aren't considering. You and the sponsor might be a perfect match!

**Finding Sponsors through Your Network**

One of my best sponsorships came through the network of friends that I have in combat sports. There was a company that was looking for exposure, and I was able to offer them the active promoting and professionalism that they were looking for, so we made a deal. I wouldn't have known about the opportunity if it hadn't been for my network so be sure to keep in touch with your network and offer value to them whenever possible. This particular opportunity came about because I had taken such good care of this person that he wanted to reciprocate my goodwill and bring an opportunity to me.

So be sure to take care of the people in your circle and look out for each other because success truly is a team sport.

**The Key to Success in Sponsorships**

There is one question that you should be asking yourself to separate yourself from the pack, "What's in it for the other guy?" Additionally, you should ask, "What do they need?" and work backwards from that. Art Davie really solidified that concept for me and the results were undeniably good.

When you're crafting your proposal, of course you're going to ask for something. But when you start by thinking about how you benefit a sponsor first, your proposal instantly gets better.

Always start relationships by providing value and showing the sponsor that you're ready to be invested in them. A great sponsorship happens when both parties want to raise each other up, but you need to set a positive tone from the beginning to make that happen.

**Sponsorship Materials Packet**

A "must have" is a good sponsorship packet that's ready to go at a moment's notice. Take your time in crafting this packet because this will speak for you when you're not around.

Make sure that your packet includes:

1. Great pictures of you working.
2. Your Cutman/Cutwoman resume (which we'll discuss in the next section).
3. Well-written, spell-checked and edited information.
4. Professional finishing by a graphic designer.

This packet should quickly and concisely explain:

1. Who you are.
2. What you'll do for the sponsor.
3. What the "ask" (discount, product, pay) is.

**The following is an excerpt from my actual sponsor packet:**

Proposal for Sponsorship of Adrian "Tenacity" Rosenbusch, Cutman for Combat Sports

*What is a Cutman?*

*"A Cutman is the professional who expertly wraps the hands of fighters before a fight in order to protect their hands from injury, who applies Vaseline on the faces of the fighters just before they enter the cage for their fights, and who stops swelling and bleeding from cuts to fighters during breaks between fight rounds so that the fighters can continue the fight.*

*Why Consider Sponsoring a Cutman?*

*As a sponsor, Cutmen are an incredible value for investment since Cutmen have many opportunities for camera time during a combat sport event. Cutmen are on camera during every stage of the fight night, from wrapping the hands of fighters before the fight, to preparing the fighters to enter the cage, to taking care of the fighters' injuries during the fight. The role of the Cutman presents a unique opportunity for a sponsor's logo to show up on camera in extended shots throughout the night.*

*Cutmen work with multiple fighters, coaches, and gyms throughout the year both in the U.S. and abroad, which means*

*that a sponsor's logo is able to reach many groups. Also, because Cutmen are in the corners supporting all of the fighters and making sure that all are able to give their best performance, the fans view Cutmen, and their sponsors, favorably.*

*Cutmen provide seminars in which their expertise is sought by those in all stages of the sport, from seasoned coaches to amateur fighters, who want to learn how to take better care of themselves. When a Cutman is sought out as an expert, the first thing people notice are the sponsor logos with which the Cutman is associated.*

*The careers of Cutmen extend for many years, which is of value to the sponsor because they are able to develop long-term relationships with fans. Through their specialized skill-set, Cutmen can also offer unique insight into product development.*

### *How Am I Unique as a Cutman?*

*As a Cutman, I am known for providing compassionate care of the highest quality to fighters during the intense experience of a fight. I possess a strong work ethic and am constantly striving to better my skills. I am meticulous and disciplined in my work and am driven by a passion for both learning and teaching. I constantly strive to advance the standards of care for fighters in combat sports. Because I enjoy helping others learn, I provide seminars and workshops on the art of being a Cutman and devote considerable effort to mentoring promising candidates in the field.*

*As a compassionate person, I am very involved in philanthropy and have worked with the following:*

- *Warrior to Warrior: Help provide outreach to homeless veterans in Las Vegas including resources for food, water, and shelter.*
- *It Ain't Chemo: Volunteer for fundraising events, wrapping hands of "Cancer Warriors" for UFC private event at UFC gym; Cutman for cancer patient, Ethan Mendenhall, for his training day at Xtreme Couture sparring with Ryan Couture.*
- *Autism Speaks: Organized a fundraiser at the Foundation Room at Mandalay Bay Casino, Las Vegas, NV.*
- *U.S. Vets: Donated goods and volunteered at the "Stand Down" Event.*
- *National MS Society and ASPCA: Donated funds and goods.*
- *Zoo Homeless Pets: Founded my own grassroots charity in Brazil: I started a grassroots charity in Sao Paulo, Brazil in which homeless pets are given life saving vaccinations and treatment at no cost to their owners.*

## *Why Sponsor Me?*

*A simple exchange of sponsorship funds for wearing a logo at events is not the defining nature of a good sponsor-brand ambassador relationship. I believe that what makes a good relationship is when both parties involved truly want to elevate the status of the other. I want to work with a brand that I am proud to be associated with and I am sure you are looking for the same thing with your brand ambassadors.*

*In my position in combat sports I am asked for advice on all facets of the game from career advice to equipment selection. This puts me in a position to align people in my industry with brands that will be an asset to them. That being said, I take the trust that is placed in me very seriously and I will not promote for financial gain brands that I do not see of value. I say that to let you know that my integrity is very important to me, and it is a large part of why I have reached my goals.*

*Should you choose to sponsor me as a Cutman, I will promote your brand with heartfelt enthusiasm such as through social media and by wearing your logo. I am also more than happy to assist with working a trade show booth or with any other promotional ventures approved by the UFC. But I feel that the real value I will provide to you comes when I am asked about your product when no one else is around. I will sincerely and enthusiastically describe the quality of your product because I feel that what will truly fire people's desire to explore your brand is the enthusiasm I impart as an experienced user of your product.*

*I hope to have an open dialogue with my sponsors and be able to express ideas to improve their brands as well as to let them know how I have been spending my time as a brand ambassador for them. I want you to be as excited about my accomplishments as I am about yours. I look forward to exploring your brand's sponsorship of me as a Cutman for Combat Sports."*


**Sponsorship Materials: Cutman/Cutwoman Resume**


This resume is not to be confused with a normal resume; sponsors don't care what your first job was, unless it's directly related to them. This is something that you need to keep updated throughout your career so that you can always give timely information to potential sponsors.


Additionally, you will need this resume if you work in certain countries in order to qualify for a work visa. You don't want to try to remember all the events you've worked after several years, trust me! I was applying for a work visa and I was asked for a Cutman resume for the last four years and I hadn't updated it for two years! That was a very late night full of looking through emails for dates, locations, and event names. So please, keep your Cutman/Cutwoman resume updated so you're ready to go.

The following is a sample layout of what your Cutman/Cutwoman resume should look like.

**Sample Cutman/Cutwoman Resume for someone who only has a few shows:**

### *Education Highlights*

- *Fight Business Academy: Professional Cutman/Cutwoman Course — Graduate*
- *Fight Business Academy: Cutman/Cutwoman Boot Camp—Certified Cutman*
- *Sports Management Worldwide Mixed Martial Arts Management Course — Graduate*

### Licensure

- *Licensed by the Nevada State Athletic Commission*
- *Licensed by the California State Athletic Commission*

### Experience

- "Boxing Event" August 25$^{th}$ 2019 Las Vegas, Nevada

- "Muay Thai Event" August 30th$^{rd}$ 2019 Las Vegas, Nevada
- "MMA Event" September 1$^{st}$ 2019 Las Vegas, Nevada
- "Boxing Event" September 25$^{th}$ 2019 Las Vegas, Nevada"Muay Thai Event" October 3$^{rd}$ 2019 Las Vegas, Nevada

**Sample Cutman/Cutwoman Resume for someone who has several years of experience:**

### *Education Highlights*

- *Fight Business Academy: Professional Cutman/Cutwoman Course—Graduate*
- *Fight Business Academy: Cutman/Cutwoman Boot Camp—Certified Cutman*
- *Sports Management Worldwide Mixed Martial Arts Management Course— Graduate*

### Licensure

- *Licensed by the Nevada State Athletic Commission*
- *Licensed by the California State Athletic Commission*
- *Licensed by CABMMA Brazilian Athletic Commission*
- *Licensed by the Australian Athletic Commission*

## *Media*

*Featured in "MMA Magazine" May 4$^{th}$ 2019 Edition*
*Featured Guest "MMA Podcast" July 4$^{th}$ 2019*
*Interview NBC 5 News "Boxing Segment" July 5$^{th}$ 2019*

## *Experience*

- "Boxing Event" August 25$^{th}$ 2018 Las Vegas, Nevada
- "Muay Thai Event" August 30th$^{rd}$ 2018 Las Vegas, Nevada
- "MMA Event" September 1$^{st}$ 2018 Las Vegas, Nevada
- "Boxing Event" August 25$^{th}$ 2019 Sao Paulo, Brazil
- "Muay Thai Event" August 30th$^{rd}$ 2019 Buenos Aires, Argentina
- "Boxing Event" September 25$^{th}$ 2019 Saint George, Utah
- "Muay Thai Event" October 3$^{rd}$ 2019 Rio De Janiero, Brazil

**Contacting a Potential Sponsor**

Most of the time sponsors prefer that you contact them by email because it's convenient and non-intrusive, but there are exceptions, so be flexible. Sometimes emails can get lost in people's shuffle. I always include my phone number in my correspondence with sponsors and encourage them to follow up by phone if they prefer, which many choose to do. At some point you'll have a phone conversation with the sponsor to go over details, but more importantly, they want to get a better sense of what kind of person you are and how well they think that you will be able to represent them.

Look at the sponsors' Website and see if there's a particular form or method of contacting them for sponsorship. If you can't find any information on how to submit sponsorship proposals, you can always call the main number on the Website and have them direct you from there.

If you are filling out a form on a Website you can usually attach a document to it, which is a great idea because you will stand out from the crowd in the best way possible.

**Pro Tip:** If the system does not allow attachments, you can always leave a download link using a site like "mediafire.com". This will enable the company to download your packet with one click, which shows that you are tech-savvy and resourceful. Keep the links to your resume and packet in a note folder on your phone for quick access; you never know when you'll need them. I've been in more than one situation where having my materials available immediately clearly put me ahead of my competition.

Choose a good time to approach your sponsor. If you have just landed an event that's only thirty days away then you will want to limit your sponsor quest to a handful of local level sponsors—unless it's an elite-level event, in which case you can pursue larger sponsors. In general, you want to approach them when you both have time to not rush anything. I've made last minute sponsorship deals that went well, so it's possible, but stressful for everyone involved.

**Pro Tip:** For elite-level/televised events, make sure that you will be able to wear the logo of your new sponsor at the event. Many televised events have restrictions on which sponsors you are allowed to wear. Check in with the person who hired you about sponsors' logos on your vest before the event.

Sponsors also like it when you pay attention to the annual business quarters when approaching them. If you are not familiar with what business quarters are, there are four groups, of three-month intervals, which make up the calendar year for businesses. The business quarters are:

Q1 January, February, March

Q2 April, May, June

Q3 July, August, September,

Q4 October, November, December.

Most businesses prefer that you contact them at least two quarters before they need to pay (for paid sponsorships). For larger sponsorship deals, it's important to contact them no later than the third quarter of the year for the first quarter of the next year. This applies mainly to paid sponsorships; product or discount sponsorships are typically more flexible.

**Pre-Contact Checklist**

Before you contact a sponsor, it is important to have all of your supporting materials and FAQs ready to go as suggested by the following checklist.

<u>Purchase a Vest</u>: Buy a "Ranger Vest" to put patches on for your events. That vest is what you see many Cutmen/Cutwomen wearing that is full of patches with logos. You can find these vests on websites such as amazon.com and ebay.com.

<u>Know Patch Sizes</u>: Know the dimensions of all the patches on your vest so that the sponsor knows what placement and size their logos will be.

<u>Determine Art Requirements</u>: Find a print shop that will make your patches for you, either in town (recommended) or online, and ask them what the art requirements are to make patches. Be sure to ask for the file format and the resolution. In my experience, it is typically 300 DPI resolution and .jpg or adobe illustrator files. If they are screen-printed you will ask to have them printed onto fabric that you provide (100% cotton is best). Then have them sewn onto patches afterwards. If you are

comfortable sewing them yourself, then you have an additional advantage.

Have a Website: Having a website dedicated to your Cutman/Cutwoman business is a great idea. You want to have an online presence for people to visit and become familiar with you and your work.

Packet Including Your Proposal: This is important because you need to give the sponsor all of the relevant information about yourself so that they are excited about you and can distribute the information within the company as needed.

This packet will include:

One page cover letter

Cutman/Cutwoman resume

Sponsorship Proposal.

Be sure to have this ready to go in a PDF document so that you are ready to deliver it quickly. Be sure it is clearly labeled for each sponsor.

Have a Cutman/Cutwoman Resume Available Separately: There are occasions when you will need a resume, separate from your packet, so be sure to have that on hand.

**Crafting Your Proposal**

When you start crafting your proposal, you need to take into account the level you are at and what you are asking for.

Take an objective view of what you are about to ask for and see if it makes sense. Are you an elite Cutman/Cutwoman asking for a discount sponsorship from a local sponsor? That might not make a lot of sense since, in that situation, you are on international TV and it is unlikely that a local sponsor would be able to get the benefit it needs from that audience. Therefore, it would not benefit that sponsor to pay you accordingly. Under those circumstances, you are only looking at paid sponsorships from companies that can benefit from international traffic to their business. For example, if you have a discount at a local tire shop, how much benefit does that tire shop get by you being on television in other countries? They might be more excited about a local MMA event where it might increase their foot traffic. By the time you're looking at working international events, you should be representing businesses that can directly benefit from international exposure.

The opposite is not quite the same. If you are working amateur events and you deliver a great proposal for a smaller compensation, then you have a chance of landing large sponsors. This is a great idea for the mindset that you can grow with your sponsors and make larger proposals with them as you reach bigger shows and more exposure.

<u>Things to include in Your Proposal to a Potential Sponsor to Set You Apart from the Crowd:</u>

- Offer to help out at your sponsor's trade show

booth as a "brand ambassador."
- Detail how many times a week you will post on social media about your sponsor's products.
- Offer to test new products and give feedback on them to your sponsor.
- Offer to host a giveaway of one of your sponsor's products on social media. (There are apps available for a small fee that will make tracking participants "likes" and "follows" easy to do.)
- Give your sponsor positive feedback on one of its products that you enjoy the most or are most interested in owning.
- Propose ways with which you could assist that are specific to the company.
- Get creative and make a proposal that fits that particular sponsor perfectly and be willing to be flexible.

**Pro Tip**

Do not make your very first approach ever to your dream sponsor. When pitching your proposal, try your second favorite sponsor first, and learn from that experience, before making your pitch to the one you're really excited about. If your second choice says "Yes" then it is definitely going to be your first favorite from now on, because they are invested in your success.

**Follow-Up**

Following up with a potential sponsor almost always means the difference between success and failure. If you do not follow up with a sponsor, the likelihood of your bid going through drops dramatically. Sponsorship proposals require effective communication and it is your responsibility to keep that communication moving along. You do not want to annoy potential sponsors with constant communication, but you also do not want to disappear off their radar. In short—the better you are at follow-up the better your chances are.

Here Is a Great General Timeline for Sponsor Follow-up:

1. Follow up in a week to see if they received your information; also ask them how you can further assist them while offering options.
2. Follow up in a month to see what questions they might have.
3. Send monthly updates of your newsletter, if you have one, or in a letter.
4. Send suggestions for new opportunities to work together. Charity events are great ways to break the ice—ask for a small sponsorship for an upcoming charity event at which you are volunteering.
5. Did your sponsor win an award or special recognition? Congratulate them! Stay invested in their success.
6. Stay positive and active on social media so that if

your sponsor checks up on you, it will see a great ambassador for its brand.

It is important to keep in mind that if your sponsor is a company you had already heard of, that is because it is working hard to build a name for itself so it is very busy. It is nothing personal, but your sponsorship is a low priority for them. They are concerned with keeping the company profitable. With that in mind, always show them ways that you are helping them become more successful.

**You got the sponsorship, now what?**

Congratulations! Your sponsorship is something to be celebrated! Be sure to take a second and enjoy this great victory.

First things first: be sure to thank your new sponsor on social media. This generates excitement about your sponsor and elevates your standing in the combat sports world.

Secondly, it is time to get artwork from your sponsor and get their logos on your vest right away! If you get a last minute gig, you want to be sure to have the logos already set.

A newsletter is a great way to stay in touch and show your sponsors that they have made a great decision in supporting you. In my personal experience, newsletters have been greatly appreciated by sponsors and, in some cases, have led to more support from my sponsors. You can release newsletters in many different intervals, including monthly or quarterly, whichever you see the best results from.

If you do not have a lot of news in the beginning, get some going! Volunteering for charity events is a great way to start some events happening while you keep pressing for more events to work. If you haven't been hired for events, you can still show up and take photos with everyone to keep current and to network. Take photos of yourself with the organizers of the show and post those to social media. Keep busy!

Always end your newsletters by acknowledging your sponsor's support and how important it is to you.

Newsletter Email Example:

*Subject: Cutman/Cutwoman Sponsorship Newsletter*

*Mr./Mrs. Smith,*

*I want to keep you in the loop about what I've been up to since we last spoke. Thank you again for everything and know that I am extremely thankful for your support. I am including my newsletter is as an attachment below.*

*I'm really happy that you're enjoying all the photos I'm putting up on Facebook and Instagram. They're getting some great reactions! I've also had a few coaches use my affiliate link, after I gave them a sample and asked them to tell me how they liked it. So thank you again for setting that up! In particular, they mentioned that they enjoyed (feature) but they wished it had (additional features). Overall, they really enjoyed it and said it was better than what they were currently using.*

*Thank you again for sending that package last week with the new (products) in it. I can't wait to use them at my next event!*

*I'm more than happy to help out at the booth you have it at the MMA Expo in September and could even do some demonstrations for attendees. I think that might even help them become more involved with your brand.*

*Thank you again for your support!*

*P.S. I mentioned you on the (MMA Example) podcast I was on last night! It's at the 3:44 minute mark. Here's a link to it (include link).*

<u>Sample Newsletter Attachment:</u>

*Hello everyone! First of all thank you to all of my sponsors! Your sponsorship is a huge help to me and I truly appreciate your continued support! This July has already been an incredible month for me. I've worked two international shows and I have several more scheduled for the rest of the year.*

*Here are the shows scheduled for the next few months, so far:*

*"Boxing Event" August 25$^{th}$ 2018, Las Vegas, Nevada*

*"Muay Thai Event" August 30 $^{th}$ 2018, Las Vegas, Nevada*

*"MMA Event" September 1 $^{st}$ 2018, Las Vegas, Nevada*

*"Boxing Event" August 25 $^{th}$ 2019, Sao Paulo, Brazil*

*I was also on the (MMA, for example) channel and I was able to discuss my sponsors in the segment. I hope you liked that! If there are talking points you'd like me to use, please let me know and I'll try my best to incorporate them.*

*As you can see on social media, my volunteer work has also kept me very busy. I'm working a charity event next month and the organizer is allowing me to wear my vest with all my sponsors' logos on it, so that's a win for everyone—especially the (beneficiaries of the event).*

*Another fun thing is that a picture of me wearing my sponsor vest was retweeted by HBO Boxing last night when I was congratulating the champion on his win! 10 million people saw your logos, so that's a great bonus!*

*I've included individual experiences for each of my sponsors in the body of the emails, so I hope you enjoy those. I'm looking forward to keeping this year going strong. Again, thank all of your for your generous support!*

*P.S. I've attached some high-resolution photos from my last event; please feel free to use them.*

**<u>Pro Tip</u>:** Most word processing software includes professional-looking templates that you can use to make your newsletter more interesting to read. This is one publication were you do not need a graphic designer to make things look nice.

**Next Steps**

Consider which sponsors you currently have and whether future sponsors would complement or compete with them. Decide which allies would be the best for you long term. Keep a long view of your sponsorship partners and be absolutely sure to treat them as valuable relationships.

There are always opportunities to level up your sponsors as you start working bigger shows. You should always weigh those possibilities on a case-by-case basis. Bigger brands have more money to work with, but might not be as flexible as you're used to—it's all in the details. See what's going to benefit you the most and which feels like a brand you're proud to represent.

Keep your eyes out for new brands that are trying to break into combat sports, they need great ambassadors to help out, and that's you!

## 22

## HOW TO HANDLE INTERVIEWS LIKE A PRO

Being professionally interviewed is something that most people are completely unprepared for in life. The most intimidating type of interview may be when a reporter sticks a microphone in your face while a bright camera light disorients you. These interviews understandably don't come off as polished as I'm sure you, the interviewee, would like. Contrast that scenario with an in-studio celebrity interview and you'll see the huge difference preparation can make.

Interviews are a great way to elevate your standing in the sport, which helps you move up to working even bigger events, that is why I have included a segment on them in this book.

. . .

My protégé, Swayze Valentine, is currently the most interviewed Cutperson in the world and, fortunately, I was careful to mentor her in the art of the interview. In this segment, I've taken the most important lessons that I shared with Swayze and refined them even further so that you can make the most of every interview you have.

Now Swayze is a polished professional who is very comfortable in front of any camera, from ESPN interviews, UFC Pay Per Views, to the TV series "Kingdom" where she plays herself.

**Publication Medium for Interview**

Interviews are usually published in one of the following mediums:

1. Print/Web Articles: magazines, sports websites, human-interest pieces

1. Radio/Podcast: local/national radio, sports podcasts, business podcasts

1. <u>Video</u>: national TV series, sports documentaries, news channels, etc.

## Types of Interviews

Publications in all of these media are interesting, but you need to prepare for the specific type of interview in which you will take part, whether by email, phone, or on-camera.

## <u>Email:</u>

Email interviews are usually the least intimidating for most people because there is less demand to be on point the entire time. Don't let the lack of urgency lull you into a false sense of security, however, since these answers will be printed with your name next to them and once it's out in the press—it's out.

1. Make sure to use spell-checking software! You don't want to be perceived as unintelligent, and some outlets will print whatever you send them without checking your grammar and spelling. Personally, I recommend looking at "Grammerly" software, it's very robust and I love using it for all my written communications.

1. Take your time! Don't hurry through the process because you are only answering a few simple questions. Give your answers some thought and write your responses in the way that best reflects who you are as a professional. That being said, don't take too long for the whole process or you run the risk of overthinking your responses.

1. Use the medium to your advantage. I've yet to run into a situation where the interviewer asked me to not to share my answers with anyone before returning them. This means that you can have someone you trust take a second look at your responses to verify that you are sending the message that you intend to send. An additional pair of eyes can really help you with the tone of your responses, in particular. This is the only medium where you'll have this advantage, so you might as well use it!

## Phone:

Phone interviews are the next step up in intensity because at least half of them are live interviews on radio shows or podcasts. Even the simple phone interviews for written articles are a big step up from email interviews.

1. Dress nicely! It may sound odd, but dressing up will improve your own confidence in your first phone interviews. After you have developed confidence in your ability to be interviewed, then you can decide if this strategy is still helpful for you.

1. Put your phone on "Do Not Disturb" after you place your call. You don't want to be a distraction during your own interview with notification sounds. If the interviewer has to ask you to silence your phone notifications during the interview you will look very unprofessional to say the least.

1. Use a wired headset for the interview, not a wireless Bluetooth headset. Bluetooth headsets are convenient when you're on the go, but they

can have some big drawbacks for interviews. One of these drawbacks is that it has to be well charged in order to work throughout the interview, and if the battery is low—most headsets will give you auditory warnings, which can make you miss a question. Clarity is another problem. I've stopped using Bluetooth headsets for meetings and interviews because the audio quality just isn't reliable. Bluetooth headsets sometimes also pick up very quiet background noises and amplify them. Stay with your phone plugged in during interviews and avoid the Bluetooth related hassles.

1. Go someplace quiet for the interview. Find a place that has as few distracting noises as possible and let people know that you have an important interview in which to participate. You don't want to have any background noise interfering with you as you deliver your message.

### On-Camera:

On-camera interviews are by far the most intimidating form of interview for most people. Even if the interview is not a live broadcast, it definitely feels like the stakes are higher.

1. <u>Looking Your Best</u>. If your on-camera interview was not a scheduled interview, it will most likely be after an event, so you will still be wearing your professional gear, which is great.

For any other on-camera interview, you will want to look your best, so here are a few tips to help you nail it.

1. Have your hair cut or styled for the interview. If you feel sharp, it will make a huge psychological impact on how you feel on camera. If you look well groomed, your interviewer will pick up on that cue and treat you differently, whether consciously or subconsciously.

1. Avoid bright whites, greens, reds, nude colors, deep blacks, and busy patterns in your clothing. These colors create a multitude of problems on camera. You should opt for blues, magentas,

browns, or greys on camera. Blacks can also work well, as long as they're not so dark that you end up looking like a silhouette.

1. Iron your clothes. Wrinkles look sloppy—end of story.

1. Wear nice shoes and socks. You don't want to find out that there is a wide shot of you and the interviewer sitting next to each other and your shoes or socks don't look good.

1. Be well rested. Cameras are extremely unforgiving when you have not gotten the proper amount of sleep. From bags under your eyes, to uneven complexion, you do not want to look exhausted. For those who are unfamiliar with make-up usage, professional broadcasters use make-up every time they are on the air, whether they are male or female. So don't be shy about using foundation if you need to.

1. For more information on selecting your clothing for an interview please read the following article from Indigo Productions:

https://www.indigoprod.com/nyc-video-production-blog/2018/05/what-to-wear-for-a-tv-interview-or-a-video-production-shoot/ by Max Rosen, President & CEO, Indigo Productions

2.<u>Sounding Your Best</u>

a. Volume! Microphones are fantastic inventions but they definitely lose a lot of the emotional intensity you are trying to communicate during a recording. You must speak with 30% more energy than you would in a normal conversation in order to accurately translate your emotional energy to the audience. Just think about how much energy an analyst or reporter uses when covering an event on television. When you hear them in person, they're using even more energy! It actually takes a great deal to come across as yelling during this type of an interview. Enunciate your words and make sure your diaphragm is fully engaged to provide the breath you need for speaking when doing an interview. Also, do not forget to project your voice energetically.

. . .

b. Kill the filler words: the "ums", "likes", "you knows", etc. These words are great examples of words that just fill up space and buy us time as we organize our thoughts. Using these words reduces your eloquence significantly. Therefore, you need to address this point if you want to be considered "well spoken."

c. Awareness is the first step. Listen to yourself speak during normal conversation and see how frequently you use unnecessary filler words. Once you've become aware of how much you use these words, you can start to eliminate them. And once you've eliminated them, you'll notice how much more eloquent you sound—and you will come across that way in interviews.

d. Pause. Instead of dropping in a filler word, take a short pause before continuing with your thought. Using this technique will make you appear mindful of what you're saying and mindful that your words carry weight. Great storytellers use this technique to tremendous effect.

e. Drinks. Your choice of beverage can greatly influence how effectively you are able to communicate during an interview. Best practices include avoiding dairy products such as, milk; sodas, juices or anything else that might have you clearing your throat during your interview. Water or herbal teas are great choices for vocal clarity.

**Control the Interview**

"If you show up at an interview and answer all of the questions, letting the interviewer dictate the pace and content of the interview the entire time, you have missed a golden opportunity." – Fight Business Academy.

Most interviewers are respectful people who are looking for great content for their audiences. They have no intention of making you look bad, but they can unintentionally put you in a tricky spot, or more commonly, a boring spot, which is just as bad. Most interviewers have done minimal research on you and have no idea what questions they might even ask a Cutperson.

Because of these possibilities, it's up to you to make the interview great. You don't do this by quickly giving clever answers and hoping the interviewer asks you the perfect question so that you can really shine. No. You accomplish this by subtly taking control of the interview for everyone's benefit.

. . .

If you do it correctly, the interviewer will have a great time interviewing you and will thank you for being such a fun guest. In this section we'll outline the two secrets to consistently creating a great interviews and never feeling stuck or panicked.

I learned these concepts from studying Chael Sonnen (whom I had the pleasure of working with on multiple occasions and whom I greatly respect). I also had these concepts reinforced by a member of his coaching staff with whom I worked. Chael was also a politician, and when comparing his methods to those of any other professional politician in front of a camera, I found that his methods were incredible. I field-tested his methods and found that they worked so incredibly well that they became my ironclad rules for interviews.

**Important:** If you forget everything else in this chapter please remember these two rules and you'll still be ahead of the game!

**The Two Golden Rules for Interviews:**

**Rule 1: Amateurs "answer" questions; Pros "handle" questions.** This rule will dictate the pace and tone of the interview right from the first question. If you answer the interviewer's question immediately, you are accepting the framework and tone of the question and therefore you are in the interviewer's full control. This is a very normal sequence for most people, but by virtue of the fact that you are reading this book, it is safe to assume that you are interested in being exceptional, not average—so let's dig in.

This rule is about how to not process interviewers questions personally and/or reactively, but instead, methodically, in order to gain a tactical advantage.

Here's a great analogy for how to handle a question versus answering a question:

If someone throws a ball to you, then you must decide whether you are going to catch it with you hands or your face. Lack of a specific action will lead to the ball hitting you in the face by default—and then you've lost control of it completely. If you opt to raise your hand instead, you will catch the ball and decide what to do with it next. This is precisely what you need to do with questions.

. . .

Don't wait until the question has sunk into your emotional core—and therefore elicits an emotional response. Catch it outside of your body where it's still an objective question. Imagine looking at it in your hand. Examine it like you would anything you find fascinating, and then decide what you feel like doing with it.

So when you are getting ready for an interview, imagine that your hand is out—literally out in front of your face—waiting to catch that question.

Keep in mind that all of this happens in a second or two, and that's perfect. Remember that slowing down sounds more deliberate and intelligent anyway, so it's not a negative. That is the key to handling a question.

Practical Exercise: "Well that's not accurate." The next time someone sends a less than friendly comment your way, instead of becoming defensive, just think: "Well that's not accurate" and move on. Safety first. (However, I would not recommend saying this phrase out loud to a crazy person who means you harm!) The point of this exercise is to train yourself to not take everything so personally and emotionally. The second you can react with, "Well that's not accurate," internally you have gained a valuable skill. This skill will help you so that you are not overly emotional in interviews and, therefore, you are not indulging knee-jerk reactions.

Story Time: I did have an altercation at a bar where an intoxicated person, whom I had not previously met, decided that I was the source of all his shortcomings in life and proceeded to challenge me to a fight. In attempting to provoke me into fighting him, he made some very unpleasant remarks about me, including a negatively worded aggressive assumption about my gender preferences in potential mates. I looked at him and replied, "Well that's not accurate," and I walked away leaving him unsatisfied and hilariously confused. He thought for sure I would fight him for saying such potentially hurtful things, but instead, I just had a great laugh and a pleasant evening. I would not recommend this course of action—this is just an amusing true story that demonstrates an extreme application of this line of thinking. Again, please don't provoke crazy people! Safety first.

"Handling" questions is a mental discipline that has to take priority over your emotions. Your emotions come into play once you have steered the question to your desired destination, which brings us to Rule #2: "Bridge to what you want to talk about."

. . .

**Rule 2: Bridge to what you want to talk about.** This is the secret sauce—where you take control of the interview and guide it to the type of interview that you really want. It takes a very stubborn interviewer to not fully indulge this tactic.

The key to bridging is to be creative. Being creative on the fly can be extremely difficult, so be patient with yourself if this doesn't come easily for you. Spend 90% of your mental focus on the first part of the bridge and then the other 10% on ramping up your energy.

You are taking a question and elevating the excitement and energy of it through the roof. Make that question a Launchpad, not a snooze fest! Here's an example:

Question: So what exactly does a Cutman do?

Bridge: As a Cutman, my job is divided into two main categories. Number 1 is wrapping the fighter's hands and the other is taking care of any damage that happens to the fighter in less than 60 seconds. (Bridge) But what most people never see is what I've seen behind the scenes, the life-altering experiences you have and incredible bonds you make. I'm there that night to immediately make a connection with a fighter and help him/her in any ethical way possible. You get to see the complete spectrum of human emotions from fear, to elation, and everything in between. Anyone can be there in the bright lights next to a winner, but it will test your soul to be there holding a fighter's hand in a hospital bed when the lights are out and everyone has gone home. So, to answer your question, I make a difference to every fighter I stand next to on any given night.

Wasn't that a much richer response than the original question suggested? That's why this is so important. Personally, I don't like pedestrian questions—I like to get into something deep and meaningful as soon as possible and, because of the bridging tactic, I can.

It's fine if the first one or two questions are simple exchanges, but it always makes for a better interview the sooner you carve your own path. If you're nervous, just try to bridge one question during the interview. Trust me when I say that that will be your favorite part of the interview when you watch it.

Even with a stubborn interviewer, you'll still get to make great points and the interviewer will come across as unnatural, not you. Keep in mind that every single time the interviewer asks you a question, you will be starting "The Two Golden Interview Rules" sequence again, and the interviewer will either struggle to maintain control of the interview or perk up and celebrate the fun, natural vibe that seemed to come out of nowhere.

Practical Exercise: Tell your friends and family that you are practicing bridging to different topics as part of your training. Have your friend or family member ask you the dullest question they can think of and practice bridging it to a topic you would love to talk about.

Make a game of it with extremely bad questions and massive bridges to completely unrelated topics. You'll struggle and sound crazy in the beginning, but you'll also be mastering a valuable skill quickly and creatively. Have fun!

Here are a few questions and bridges to get you started:

Question: What's your favorite color?

Bridge: What it takes to become a great Cutman/Cutwoman.

. . .

Question: Who's that guy? (Pointing to some random person)

Bridge: Why UFC/HBO/Showtime/etc. should hire you.


Question: Why's my foot asleep?

Bridge: Why becoming a Cutman/Cutwoman is important to you.


Question: Do you think Godzilla is nice in real life?

Bridge: Are you crazy?! That's an amazing question! Answer it!!!


<u>Gotcha and Inappropriate Questions</u>: This is what most people are terrified about when they are asked to do an interview—and understandably so. Some interviewers like to stir up controversy on their show in order to get more interest in their shows—and it frequently works.


In order to not get frozen in your tracks and run over, you must adhere to the "Two Rules for Interviews," section above.

. . .

When the inflammatory question is asked, you must immediately handle that question.

Important: Never let the interviewers see that they've rattled you. They're going to be taking cues from you after they ask their question.

Here's an example of how to handle an absurd "gotcha" question:

Interviewer: Hi Adrian! Thank you for joining us. Let's cut right to it. Many people have decided that you're solely responsible for the extinction of several species, what do you have to say?

Me: Yeah I heard that one, but it's not nearly as good as the one where I'm single handedly responsible for global warming—I don't even understand the logistics of that one. I wish people would focus on the real struggles that I have to deal with, those are way more interesting, such as...(dealing with the stigma of a head injury, lewd comments because I teach women, the resistance I've gotten opening up Fight Business

Academy, or anything else I actually want to talk about).


Interviewer: Ha Ha! I hadn't heard that one. So tell me more about...


Here's an example of how to handle an "inappropriate" question. Ladies please pay extra special attention because you are statistically more likely to receive these, just ask any female celebrities.


Interviewer: Hi Cutwoman! Thank you for joining us. I heard that the only reason you got into the UFC is because you secretly dated Dana White, is that true?


Cutwoman: That question is exactly what's wrong with this industry, because it might be directed at me today, but it's really about all women in the sport no matter what their role. We've struggled just to get in this sport and then we rose to the pinnacle, thanks to the efforts of some extraordinary women and the courage of Dana White and the UFC to include us on the biggest stage on earth.

. . .

I'm too busy paving the way for the little girl in the stands to worry about the cowards who hope I fail. (Prepared sound bite)

In reality, I get so much love from fans that it's unbelievable. I'd like to take a moment to thank you guys for all the wonderful emails and the tagged photos at cage side at events. Thank you and I love you guys!

I'd also like to take one second to encourage any woman who wants to do this—to go for it! You can reach out to me if you'd like any pointers, or just go to online.fightbusinessacademy.com to get a jump-start. This is your life, only you get to decide how amazing it is!

Interviewer: That's interesting! Tell me more about your training.

That example demonstrates how to use the two golden interview rules and set a more positive tone for the rest of the interview. Of course, you can also just say, "That's an inappropriate question. Next question please," and move on. Personally, I like to turn dead-ends into opportunities, so I prefer to talk it out most of the time.

· · ·

In summary, always remember the two golden rules:

Rule 1: Amateurs "answer" question; Pros "handle" questions.

Rule 2: Bridge to what you want to talk about.


**Canned Responses: When to use them.**


The more you get interviewed the more you'll see that interviewers frequently ask the same questions. Because of this, it's important to have some well-prepared answers ahead of time. Here are a few questions you should have prepared answers for:


Q: So why did you decide to become a Cutman/Cutwoman?

A:


Q: What's the worst cut you've ever had?

A:


For the first two questions you need to find your own answers; for the second two, I'll give you some examples:

. . .

Q: Do you have to have a license to do this?

A: Licensing is up to each individual governing body for the geographical area you are in. In the United States, licensing is typically at the state level, but in other countries, it can be at the national level. It all depends on where you are in the world.


Q: So are you a Doctor or EMT?

A: I get asked this question frequently because people find Cutpeople to be so mysterious. In truth, we are part of a fighter safety team that requires ringside physicians, EMT's, Athletic Commission Inspectors, and Cutmen and Cutwomen to work together to cover all the necessary areas. Being a Cutperson requires a very specialized set of skills that are unique in the fighter safety team. Doctors and EMTs frequently take Cutman training if they want to make the transition, because there is limited overlap.


So take your time—and don't reinvent the wheel each time you're asked a standard question. You should have these answers ready to go at a moment's notice, especially if you are tired at the end of a show and someone asks you for an on the spot interview.

· · ·

**Think in "Sound Bites"**

Whenever you see an interview with a celebrity or other person who really shines on camera, you'll notice that they always have a few quotable moments. The real pros don't just hope that something catchy and magical comes out of their mouths, instead they plan one or two key moments that they want to capitalize on. Once they're in the position to deliver these gems, they make the interview golden by delivering them at the perfect time with flawless delivery.

So what exactly is a sound bite? A sound bite is a short clip from your interview that can easily stand on it's own. A great sound bite sets the entire tone of your interview in the shortest time possible. Movie trailers are masterful at this art form so you can definitely take a few cues from them. Great sound bites are thought provoking and can start a lot of conversations about your interview.

You might be thinking that you've seen someone throw in a "canned" response and it was tacky, maybe it was. The biggest difference was the timing and delivery of the line.

If you're waiting for the perfect opportunity to say a great line, you'll almost always throw it out in a disingenuous manner. You must control the interview to the greatest of your ability in order to deliver effectively.

Two tips when delivering your sound bite:

1. Speak confidently.

1. Don't look to the interviewer for validation of your point while you literally hold your breath. That habit will make you look either "soft" or like you're trying to sneak something by everyone.

A great number of sound bites in the fight industry could be categorized as "trash talking" such as:

"He'll never make it out of the first round"

"Saturday night I'm going to retire her!"

. . .

These are fine for fighters who have chosen this method to promote their fights, but being this confrontational as a Cutman or Cutwoman usually doesn't translate well. I have to mention this because I've actually seen it happen with a handful of aspiring Cutmen, and it was not well received.

As a Cutperson, your sound bites should always try to accomplish one of the following objectives with the audience:

Show that you're knowledgeable.

Build rapport.

Encourage them to like you.

Make them think you're funny.

Show them you are insightful.

Help them know you're compassionate.

. . .

Be sure to inject some passion into your viewpoints! There is nothing worse than a boring interview.

**Warning:** Some interviewers will try to lure you into saying something inflammatory just to boost their ratings and then turn that into a sound bite for promotion. Don't say anything you don't mean just to be momentarily liked in an interview.

**Summary**

I know we've covered a lot in this part of the book, but it's all going to make a huge difference when you land your first interview. I wanted to make sure that you have all my hard-earned advice on hand for when that time comes.

With all of these lessons in hand, you'll know exactly what you need in order to prepare for an interview correctly so that you not only capitalize on the interview —but you truly enjoy them! So when your first, or your next interview is on the way, take another look at this chapter and have some fun!

Photo credit Joe Piccirillo / Joe Pic Photography

## 23

## HOW TO CATCH A BREAK IN COMBAT SPORTS

---

"Luck is what happens when preparation meets opportunity"

— SENECA

---

Now that you've worked your first professional event, you are entering into an area that requires more strategic planning. Depending on what your end goal is, you need to start really narrowing your focus toward what you truly want. It's fine if you're not working every single weekend, but always try to add more regular shows to your schedule.

Consistency is key here: if you're out of sight, you'll be out of mind.

When there's a fight coming up, make sure that you're ready to work that night even if you're not scheduled to work. Being prepared and at the right place at the right time can lead you to great success.

**For MMA:**

Show up at the events that you're interested in, as long as they're not elite-level events (because you won't get very far). Introduce yourself to the promoter and the Cut-people and be available on-call to help out. Don't try to leverage yourself between the existing Cut-people and the promoter—that comes across as sleazy to everyone and will begin a negative reputation for you. Any event that only has two Cut-people needs more, so there's room to create a position for yourself. When you're discussing it with the event promoter, you can use the UFC as an example, and gently remind them that the UFC has more than two Cut-people at one show to protect the show's interests.

. . .

To sell your services, here are some benefits to having a third or fourth Cutman/ Cutwoman for a promotion:

- Everyone gets their hands wrapped properly;

- Fewer broken hands, less medical expense;

- Show has an easier time staying on schedule;

- Existing Cut-people are able to take breaks if they want;

**Tip:** The high-level message you want to communicate to the promoter is that you can solve problems for them, not create new problems.

**For Boxing/Muay Thai:**

. . .

Getting a break in these sports relies very heavily on proximity. It's unlikely that these athletes will reach out to you directly, so it's up to you to be visible. For these two Combat Sports, it's important to have the coaches trust you personally. If the coaches have mega-stars in their camp, they'll be extremely protective of those athletes, and rightfully so, because it can be a tricky industry. Volunteering to work with a gym's' amateur fighters, in order to demonstrate your skill and ability to work with the team, is one strategy.

Another strategy that should be considered is joining the gym that you want to work with. Assuming you have the time and money to join the gym, you need to ask yourself whether this course is still one you should take. The upside is that you'll be more likely to be viewed as one of their own, so they'll trust you more quickly. The downside is that you've tethered yourself to one gym, so you now have a very clear bias towards that gym. This strategy has worked in multiple sports, but cannot be officially endorsed by Fight Business Academy due to the conflicts of interest it generates. You will need to consider your own personal goals and objectives before taking this action.

Boxing is very unique in that, at the highest levels, you'll typically only work for a few fighters in your career.

These fighters have higher fight purses than other Combat Sports. They'll contract with you to pay you a percentage of the purse for your work. It is because of this that you won't need as many different gigs to be profitable. Be warned that this is an extremely competitive field and that you'll need to work every angle you see to make it happen.

**Interesting note:** The highest paid Cutmen in boxing work for less than five fighters total in a given year. The top one percent of Cutmen work for only one fighter as their main source of income.

**<u>Be ready for success</u>!** Are you actually ready for the next level? Time to do a quick self-assessment. Elite level shows and fighters are going to want to know that you actually have the experience that they need. You don't want to get in front of the right people and not be ready to back up your enthusiasm.

Make sure your Cutman/Cutwoman resume is looking good. How many amateur fights have you worked? How many Pro fights have you worked? More importantly, what was the quality of the show and where was it? Working 10 amateur events in the fight capital of the world, Las Vegas, carries a lot more weight than 10 shows in rural areas. Working 10 professional events that most people have never heard of doesn't carry as much weight as working 3 popular events.

After a show in Brazil I sat next to legendary UFC Matchmaker, Joe Silva, and I thought it would be interesting to see what he was looking for when scouting for talent. He told me that he wanted fighters that fought tough opponents and won. He didn't seem impressed by people racking up a ton of victories against fighters nobody had ever heard of. I completely agree. The reason I mention that conversation is because it's the same for a Cutman or Cutwoman. People want to see you thriving in good promotions and working with bigger fighters all the time. If you're in front of a decision maker and they ask what shows you've worked, you need to have impressive answers, not hype.

## 24

## THE CALL

Boom! You got "The Call." Most likely your mentor or another one of your close contacts introduced you to someone who decided that your resume and reputation were sufficient to give you your big break and try you out at your first major event. This is a combination of you being a true professional, as well as, the event needing someone right at that moment. Time to put on your gear and get ready for something incredible!

Have all of your critical questions in hand and don't bother the person you're communicating with after you have asked them. Part of being professional is being concise and respectful of people's time and energy. Here's that list of questions you need to know:

What is the call time and location?

Where do I get my credentials?

Who do I report to?

Who will pay me and when? *(Unless it's an audition for MMA.)*

That's all the information you need, anything else will take up too much time and energy from a very busy executive. Show up ready to work 30 minutes before your call time. You need to remember that at elite-level events, you'll most likely appear on camera, so be well groomed.

First things first: remember to double check that your license will be current during the event. If you're not licensed for that jurisdiction, submit your application ASAP in a large envelope, and call the sanctioning body two days after you've submitted it to ensure that they've received it.

**Here's what you should wear:**

Black pants with no logos (preferably EMT/Paramedic/First Responder pants)

Black shoes with no logos (or black logos)

Plain black T-Shirt with no print

Your Cutman/Cutwoman Vest with all the logos removed

(Visit www.fightbusinessacademy.com for more details)

**Here's what you should bring:**

*The Secret Roadmap for World-Class Cutmen and ...*    147

All your equipment in a roller bag;

Hand-wrap gear in a small portable bag;

2 fine-tipped permanent markers;

2 ballpoint pens;

Seconds' license;

Drivers' license;

Passport (If you're working outside of your home country. If so, you might need a Visa too.)

Snacks and water (if permitted).

All of this information is what has been universally accepted in every event I've been hired for in every country I've worked in. That being said, things can change, particularly during televised events, so show up ready to be flexible. Remember that even though this is serious work, and it will test you, this is also incredibly cool and fun!

Photo credit Joe Piccirillo / Joe Pic Photography

## 25

## QUOTES TO GUIDE YOUR CAREER

Throughout your career as a Cutman/Cutwoman you will inevitably run into adversity, and I've had the great honor to help some wonderful people in their times of need. I wanted to include some of the most helpful pieces of advice I've collected or developed on my journey. On this list, I've only included the advice that I felt has made the biggest impact.

**Fight Business Academy's Number One Rule:**

---

> "When you make a mistake you must immediately forgive yourself and move on. If you don't, then you'll snowball and spiral out of control. Learn from your mistakes, don't make the same one twice."

— ADRIAN ROSENBUSCH

**Important Quotes from Art Davie:**

"Making mistakes is a natural part of learning and an essential part of your progression. Mistakes can, and will happen, because we're human beings. How we view and manage our little failures is what will ultimately define us."

"Life is a team sport. Human beings are pack or herd animals. We rely on relationships, alliances, marriages, partnerships, corporations. We rely on these things to allow us to make life happen for us."

— ART DAVIE, CREATOR AND CO-FOUNDER OF THE ULTIMATE FIGHTING CHAMPIONSHIP. (RECORDED DURING AN INTERVIEW WITH FIGHT BUSINESS ACADEMY.)

If you're making up a list of dream mentors, Art Davie should be at the top of your list. His advice completely changed the way I look at the business side of MMA. Think about the following quote. It means you aren't expected to accomplish all of this on your own. You must form a network of strong relationships in order to prosper. I have to thank my incredible network of friends and my partnerships for all the opportunities they have brought my way. I forged my own path in this field, but the huge breaks came from all the wonderful people in my life.

---

> "Professionalism is to understand what the standards are that create greatness in anything. Whether you're a dentist or a fighter, if you understand the standards that create the highest level of performance in an area, and you then decide to follow the path necessary to create those standards for yourself, then you are expressing what I call professionalism....."

> "...Looking at what has made someone successful in an area that you wish to excel in is an excellent practice. There are some universal keys to success that apply to any field, but there are also standards

for your particular field that you need to adopt as your personal goals."

> — Art Davie, Creator and Co-founder of the Ultimate Fighting Championship. (Recorded during an Interview with Fight Business Academy).

---

For more wisdom from Art Davie, buy his book "*Is This Legal?*" (Available at Amazon.com).

**Additional Quotes to Guide Your Career:**

---

"Early is on time, on time is late, and late doesn't exist."

> — Adrian Rosenbusch

---

"Human life is truly a short affair. It is better to live doing the things that you like. It is foolish to live within this dream of a world seeing unpleasantness and doing only things that you do not like."

> — Tsunetomo Yamamoto, Hagakure: The Book of the Samurai

---

---

"Flesh is flesh and bone is bone, how famous someone is doesn't change their anatomy."

Adrian Rosenbusch

---

**Note:** I've shared the above advice when people are intimidated about the level of event they're about to work. Being around superstar athletes can be intimidating at first, so it's important to have a coping mechanism on hand.

---

> It is not the critic who counts; not the man who points out how the strong man stumbles, or where the doer of deeds could have done them better. The credit belongs to the man who is

actually in the arena, whose face is marred by dust and sweat and blood; who strives valiantly; who errs, who comes short again and again, because there is no effort without error and shortcoming; but who does actually strive to do the deeds; who knows great enthusiasms, the great devotions; who spends himself in a worthy cause; who at the best knows in the end the triumph of high achievement, and who at the worst, if he fails, at least fails while daring greatly, so that his place shall never be with those cold and timid souls who neither know victory nor defeat."

— Theodore Roosevelt, April 23, 1910.

---

That quote by Roosevelt is one of my favorites because it's such an iconic quote and it directly relates to Combat Sports. Unfortunately, in this day and age, the idea of the "troll" or "hater" is something for which people in the spotlight need strategies and support. It's difficult to create something, but it's easy for someone else to tear it down. When you start working bigger shows, you will start to attract attention, mostly good, but inevitably some bad. There's only one way to avoid the unpleasant part of the business, which leads me to my next favorite quote.

---

> "Never let anyone make you feel like you don't deserve to be here."
>
> — UFC Icon Ronda Rousey

---

This was a quote that Ronda Rousey gave to me when I asked her if she had any advice for Swayze Valentine as she pushed to become the first Cutwoman in the UFC. Swayze has treasured those words ever since.

---

> "There is only one way to avoid criticism: do nothing, say nothing, and be nothing."
>
> — Aristotle

---

So now that I've taken you on the journey from Day 1 to Elite-level Promotions what's next?

## 26

## NEXT STEPS IN YOUR JOURNEY

After absorbing all of this material, it's a good time to visualize yourself doing this work. If this feels right to you, then you owe it to yourself to go for it. Life is entirely too short to look back at the end of your days and wonder "What if?"

Pursuing this journey is one of hard work, but the payoff is incredible. You'll have stories and experiences that most people will never have in their entire lives.

This book was written to show the entire journey from Day 1 to the Elite-level, but if your goals are somewhere in the middle, that won't make this book any less useful to you. At Fight Business Academy we support our students no matter what level of events feels right for them. If your goal is to have your friends see you on pay-per-view events, then that's a great goal. If your idea of being fulfilled is to help out friends or family members at their fights, then that is also great! There's no right answer for everyone, so just do what will make you happy.

In the past, the only way to be trained in this profession was to seek out a qualified mentor to show you the proper way to do everything. You hoped they were giving you good advice, hoped they even had the time or interest to teach you, and then hoped that they had a complete plan to make sure you knew what you need to know to work as a professional. There are some phenomenal Cutmen and Cutwomen working in the field today who have extremely valuable insights to share with a potential student. The problem is, that educating students is not their focus, so they often unintentionally exclude a substantial amount of information that is second nature to them.

All of this also requires you to live in close proximity to a qualified professional who's able to meet with you consistently or for you to go to a one-time seminar with maybe a few follow-up emails, or, if you're super-lucky, a follow-up phone call. This has been the status quo for education in the Cutman/Cutwoman field and many other Combat Sports positions.

It is because of this very issue that "Fight Business Academy" was created. We are here to offer a complete education for this career and, soon, for all the other amazing careers in Combat Sports that don't offer formalized training or don't require additional training to enter the workspace as a professional. Fight Business Academy solves all of the issues that used to stand in the way of an eager student receiving his/her education.

Now, no matter where you live, what your schedule is, or what your budget is, you can learn what the elite professionals know. Fight Business Academy is developing online offerings that will give you access to all the information you need to start your journey on incredible paths.

Our online course is the result of months of preparation and ten years of experience. Our experts at Fight Business Academy are putting all of their collective information into these options and we're very excited to soon share them all with you! Our digital products are designed to give everyone the information they need to start working local events and building their foundation of experience. If that's your goal, then that's fantastic and we applaud you for wanting to learn the proper way to take care of the fighters on which you'll be working.

We are very proud of the online courses we are developing, but we've also designed something else that the Combat Sports industry has never seen before. Fight Business Academy now offers the most complete educational experience in any Combat Sport, our Cutman/Cutwoman Bootcamp! Live training in the Fight Capital of the World, Las Vegas, Nevada, at the Fight Business

Academy headquarters with our world-class instructors! This is the crown jewel of Fight Business Academy and we are so excited to be able to offer it to the public!

We have designed the most complete educational experience in the Combat Sports World and we are constantly trying to make it even better because we strongly believe that everyone must continually work to improve, to be a better version of themselves. If working in the Combat Sports industry is what you daydream about, or if you're already in the industry and you want to be the absolute best version of yourself that you can be, then it's time to join the Fight Business Academy family.

If you want to be able to learn how to provide the best care in the world to fighters when they need a skilled professional, then this Fight Business Academy is perfect for you. Professionals who work at the highest levels in MMA, Muay Thai, and Boxing designed this course. These are the real skills, techniques, and knowledge you need to be successful in the world of professional Combat Sports.

Upon completion of this online course for MMA, students will be able to:

- Know how to properly use all the tools of the trade;
- Have a working knowledge of how to keep themselves and the athletes safe;

- Give proper care to an injured athlete;
- Thrive in the world's biggest events;
- Gain inside information on what the top pros in Combat Sports are doing and why;
- Have the knowledge and skills needed to work their dream events.

Our students include:

- Passionate fans who are interested in making a career in Combat Sports;
- Cutmen/Cutwomen who aren't currently working at the highest levels of MMA, Muay Thai, and Boxing;
- Professional coaches and fighters looking to add all the skills of a professional Cutman/Cutwoman to their arsenal;
- Doctors, nurses, and all Emergency Medical Personnel looking to find fight business specific training so they can hit the ground running in Combat Sports.

*Scan with your smartphone QR Reader to go to Fight Business Academy Online Training*

## 27

## SOURCES

Tsunetomo Yamamoto, *Hagakure: The Book of the Samurai,* p. 64 William Scott Wilson (Translator) (p. 4). Accessed 22 July 2018.

Benjamin Franklin, Quotes. https://www.goodreads.com/quotes/1270715. Accessed 22 July 2018.

Nakano, Chelsi. VARK model, https://blog.prezi.com/the-four-different-types-of-learners-and-what-they-mean-to-your-presentations-infographic/. Accessed 22 July 2018.

Fleming, Neil. (2001.) Teaching and Learning Styles: VARK Strategies. My Book

Note: Currently unavailable.

Pauk, W. & Owens, R. *How to Study in College,* Eleventh Edition.

*Cornell Note Taking System*

*https://www.umfk.edu/learning-center/studying-tips/notes/*

Anders Ericsson Interview with David Burkus *Inc. Magazine.* 6-7-2016.

*https://www.inc.com/david-burkus/what-malcolm-gladwell-missed-about-the-10000-hour-rule.html*

Dunlosky J, et al. "Improving Students' Learning With Effective Learning Techniques: Promising Directions From Cognitive and Educational Psychology," *Psychological Science in the Public Interest,* 2013,14(1) 4-58.

https://www.ernweb.com/educational-research-articles/learning-techniques-effective-study/

Frank, Thomas. "How to Remember More of What You Learn with Spaced Repetition" https://collegeinfogeek.com/spaced-repetition-memory-technique[8]

. . .

Pan, S. C. (2015). The Interleaving Effect: Mixing It Up Boosts Learning. *Scientific American.* https://www.scientificamerican.com/article/the-interleaving-effect-mixing-it-up-boosts-learning/ https://effectiviology.com/interleaving/


Waitley, Denis. "The Secret." Directed by Drew Heriot. Written by Rhonda Byrne, Executive Producer, Paul Harrington. Prime Time Productions, 2007.


Chekhov, Anton. https://www.goodreads.com/quotes/7229990-knowledge-is-of-no-value-unless-you-put-it-into


Gladwell, Malcolm. 2008. *Outliers.* Little Brown and Company.


Anders Ericsson Interview with David Burkus Inc. Magazine. 6-7-2016.

*https://www.inc.com/david-burkus/what-malcolm-gladwell-missed-about-the-10000-hour-rule.html*


Maxwell, John C. http://www.wiseoldsayings.com/authors/john-c.-maxwell-quotes/

https://digitalpromise.org/2015/02/07/five-learning-strategies-that-work/

Sheepdog Response. https://sheepdogresponse.com/about/

https://www.goodreads.com/author/show/4918776.Seneca

Davie, Art & Wheelock, Sean. 2014. *Is This Legal? The Inside Story of the First UFC from the Man Who Created It.*

Tsunetomo Yamamoto, *Hagakure*: The Book of the Samurai, p. 64 William Scott Wilson (Translator) (p. 4). Accessed 22 July 2018.

Theodore Roosevelt. April 23, 1910.

Rousey, Ronda.

Aristotle.

**About the Author**

Photo Credit Matthew Lotter

Adrian "Tenacity" Rosenbusch is a world-renowned professional Cutman from Las Vegas, Nevada, who has made a career working the highest profile events around the globe.

Adrian has earned his reputation as a world-class instructor through his international seminars, guest speaking, interviews, and mentorship of the next generation of elite-level professionals. Adrian's students have proven to be the best new professionals in the industry by consistently working high profile events after training with him.

Adrian's most recognized student is his protégé, Swayze "The Queen of Cuts" Valentine, who has earned her place in history as the first and only Cutwoman to work for the Ultimate Fighting Championship.

**Career Highlights:**

Cutman for the Following Events:

The Ultimate Fighter 14 Finale, Las Vegas, United States

Season 1 The Ultimate Fighter Brazil

Season 2 The Ultimate Fighter Brazil

Season 3 The Ultimate Fighter Brazil

The Ultimate Fighter Live Team Cruz vs Team Faber

The Ultimate Fighter The Smashes: Team Australia vs Team UK

The Ultimate Fighter Nations: Team Canada vs Team Australia

The Ultimate Fighter Finale: Smashes Finale, Gold Coast, Australia

UFC on FX 7 Belfort x Bisbing, Sao Paulo, Brasil

UFC on FX 8 Belfort x Rockhold, Jaguará Do Sul, Brasil

UFC 163 Aldo x Korean Zombie, Rio De Janeiro, Brasil

UFC 164 Henderson vs Pettis, Milwaukee, United States

UFC on Fuel TV Nogueira x Werdum, Fortaleza, Brasil

UFC Fight Night Machida x Mousasi, Jaguará Do Sul, Brasil

UFC Fight Night Glover x Bader, Belo Horizonte, Brasil

UFC 166 Velasquez vs Dos Antos III, Houston, United States

UFC Fight Night Shogun x Henderson 2, Natal, Brasil

UFC 172 Jones vs Teixeira, Baltimore, United States

The Ultimate Fighter Brasil Season 3 Finale, Miocic x Maldonado, Sao Paulo, Brasil

UFC Fight Night Maia vs LaFlare, Rio De Janeiro, Brasil

UFC Fight Night Miocic vs Hunt, Adelaide, Australia

UFC 179 Aldo vs Mendes 2, Rio De Janeiro, Brasil

UFC Fight Night Shogun x Saint Preux, Uberlandia, Brasil

The Ultimate Fighter: A Champion will be Crowned, Las Vegas, United States

UFC Fight Night Machida x Dollaway, Barueri, Brasil

UFC 187 Johnson vs Cormier, Las Vegas, United States

UFC Fight Night Bigfoot x Mir, Porto Alegre, Brasil

UFC Fight Night Condit vs Alves, Goiânia, Brasil

UFC 190 Rousey x Corriea, Rio De Janeiro, Brasil

ESPN/Top Rank Boxing Friday Night Fights, Suzy Howard and Jonathan Alcantara

HBO/Golden Boy Boxing: Khan vs. Maidana, Team Tompkins

Showtime/Goldenboy/Shaw/Dibella/Mayweather Productions Ishe Smith vs Irving Garcia

Instruction:

Adrian has demonstrated his ability to teach at the highest level: Adrian's protégé is Swayze "The Queen of Cuts" Valentine. Swayze achieved international recognition when she earned her place in history as the first Cutwoman in the UFC. Adrian now focuses on teaching the next generation of Cutmen/Cutwomen so that fighters all over the world can be in the hands of professionals who have top-level training.

# ACKNOWLEDGMENTS

Photo credit Joe Piccirillo / Joe Pic Photography

Huge congratulations to the most interviewed Cutperson in the world, Swayze Valentine. You're a true inspiration!

www.ingramcontent.com/pod-product-compliance
Lightning Source LLC
Chambersburg PA
CBHW031112080526
44587CB00011B/936